Mona-Vated

Mona-Vated

Mona Arora

The LightWorks Publishing
Spirituality . Wellness . Self
TheLightWorksPublishing.com

The LightWorks Publishing
Spirituality . Wellness . Self
TheLightWorksPublishing.com

Published by:
The LightWorks Publishing
G-125 Jeevan Niketan,
New Delhi-110087 INDIA

Copyright © Mona Arora, 2016

All rights reserved. No part of this book may be reproduced or transmitted in any form or by any means without written permission of the author.

First Published: February 2016

Foreword

When I attended Mona's workshop 1st time in 2011, I was completely blown away! Despite having the good fortune of attending many transformative workshops since we started The NewAge Foundation in 2006, I was completely Blown Away!!

I always say if you were to attend ONLY one workshop in your life then THIS is the One! In just 3 days the Transformation is so complete that you become An Automatic Manifestation Magnet!

When we become enlightened to a new way of thinking, it's easy to believe that devouring all the information we can about it, will translate to the results we want.

In the case of Law of Attraction (LOA), millions around the world have been inspired by the teachings, speakers, and other mediums dedicated to it. Many have taken the first steps to changing the way they perceive life, in order to achieve goals, enhance prosperity, or simply be happier. With so many people doing so, why is it that so few see the positive change they want?

Mona's three-day experiential workshop will help you understand *exactly* why you're not seeing the changes you want even though you think you're following every rule to the letter, or reading all the right books. This workshop will change the state of your being to automatically achieve results and to get a glimpse of what you'll be experiencing; here are some of the things you'll learn about:

Focus on Feelings

How do you feel right now? Consider this for a moment and answer honestly. You see, a major part of LOA garnering success in your life, is based on feeling. Still, much of the material on the subject—while valuable—puts greater emphasis on thoughts, or continuously visualizing or constantly affirming the results you want in order to see success.

Feelings, positive or negative, are fuelled by our thoughts. When we are conflicted or are too focused on negative thoughts, this is perpetuated in our behaviour and life-view. In the same way, positive thoughts inspire happy feelings which promote vibrations that embrace the goodness around us.

When we first begin learning about Law of Attraction, we are often bogged down with the desire to ensure that each of our thoughts is positive. It's even worse on those days that seem to just not be going our way and we worry ourselves sick because our thoughts might not exactly be the best. Consider this: If we're so busy fretting and fighting to have positive thoughts, to the point where we induce anxiety and fear within, how are we supposed to feel good? **The answer is, we won't.**

We can *think* about getting that new job all day long, but if we don't *feel* we're going to get it, we're doing the opposite of what we want to achieve. What we are thinking must match up with what we are feeling, especially as attraction is primarily rooted in feelings. The more we battle ourselves to produce good thoughts, effectively bringing on frustration in the process, the further away we go from what we actually want.

It's the same with positive affirmations, which are a great way to have a continuous focus on the things you want to manifest in your life. However, repeating affirmations and not believing—feeling—they're actually going to happen, is like telling a dog to sit, then giving it a treat when it doesn't listen.

Life is not always a smooth ride and we will face challenges along the way. These mustn't be turned into reasons to abandon your desire to maintain positive thoughts and feelings. When the bad ones filter through, try to focus on something good, something that makes you laugh, or feel warm inside. More importantly, **stay away from those things that promote bad thoughts and feelings in your life.**

In Mona's workshop, you'll gain a better understanding on how to focus more on feelings, instead of just constantly thinking and visualizing results. You'll learn the importance of doing things that make you feel great as a way to curb those negative feelings. The wonderful thing is that the more you do it, even when you have bad days it won't affect you as much as before, because you'll be ready to combat it with your legion of positive energy—those things that inspire and edify.

Something's Always Happening

Before you started on the path to learning about Law of Attraction, what was going on in your life? You were working, going to school, chilling with friends, whatever you were doing, life was passing by day-by-day, not stopping for you or anyone else at any time. Now you know about LOA and you're completely taken by the principles, you feel good, things are looking up, and there's constant positive progress in your life. Then all of a sudden, a day passes, or a month or maybe even three, where it seems like that's all stalled. You think to yourself, "Isn't this working anymore? I've done everything I'm supposed to." The answer is **Law of Attraction *never* stops**.

It feels incredible when everything lines up for us. There are days when we see dreams we've worked on for years finally coming to fruition and it's all we can do to contain the excitement. When we don't get that same high at every turn, with every new move, business venture or so on, it can be easy to feel like we've failed. Like it was a one-off, or that our time in the sun was great, but now it's over. The problem with being this way is that inevitably we start giving in to bad thoughts, which in turn promote negative feelings and can interrupt us from getting what we want.

Mona will explain, how you can deal with these feelings when they come on. We'll delve into the importance of striving for good feelings even when we don't feel like it, and why it's so necessary to always try to be in a good frame of mind, so we're ready to take on self-imposed negativity.

The Importance of Feeling Good

You may be noticing a recurring theme by now that is strongly based on allowing ourselves to feel good, as a way to really manifest what we want.

Each of us needs to take particular actions in order to achieve the positive results we crave. For a cook who wants to be a great chef, it might be trying a difficult recipe each day, for a singer who wants to be famous, it could be taking voice lessons five times a week to improve their talent, and so on. As you read this you're probably thinking about the action *you* take in your quest to reach your goals.

Often though, we convince ourselves that to get what we want, it doesn't matter if these actions make us feel bad. We tell ourselves our climb up the career ladder is necessary, even though it's stressing us out. We make ourselves believe we can't quit something we hate, because we've been doing it for years. In so doing, we're actually **pushing ourselves *away* from our goals**.

In her workshop, you'll find out how to make sure your actions are not only promoting good results, but making you *feel* good too. You'll realise that it's alright to stop those things that negatively affect you, and that you'll actually speed up the train to manifestation lane, by simply focusing on feeling good.

As we grow, it takes time to get rid of the old beliefs that we so ardently held onto over the course of our lives. We can easily find ourselves reverting to actions, thoughts, and feelings that we would rather not, just **because we're not *completely* changed**—not quite yet. Imagine then how much more difficult we make this for our emerging selves, when we continuously try to 'convert' others, or make them understand this wonderful feeling we have all because of something called LOA. "Wait what now?" You've heard that before too right?

Mona not only empowers you to continue on your new path, arming you with the tools necessary to truly understand and utilize LOA, but you'll also learn how to avoid doubters who will rain on your parade and could even make you give up on your new, successful life.

I can say that Mona is just not a Coach, She lives what she teaches. Her life's story is a of great inspiration and motivation. Read this book not like a story book but to inspire yourself to become what the universe created you for...

Sandeep Goswamy
Founder
The NewAge Foundation
www.TheNewAgeFoundation.org

Preface

Dear Readers,

I appreciate that you picked up this book from a lot of hundreds available in the market. Each writing is Unique as each individual brings his unique energy unto the piece of paper. I have deep regard and appreciation for all those who have made the initiative to write, even once in their life.

Books are a piece of Art. Each book that we purchase since Childhood holds a really important place in our life. It not only added more to our wisdom and knowledge but also brings us closer to real time Stories that exist around.

I always believe that we need to have a very strong reason to pen down our feelings and then share it with rest of the world. Unless you have been moved emotionally and mentally, you will not feel motivated enough to write and share.

As humans, we are built with the feelings such as Compassion and Empathy. These are two strong and overwhelming States of Mind. The moment we feel Compassion, love, or Empathy, we are drawn towards serving the mankind in best possible manner.

I feel the reason for writing this book is the same. Mona's journey automatically asked to write a book on her Life Journey! Nothing forced her as such. But she surely went through some tough situations in Life where she felt emotionally weak and stirred by circumstances. She over came the situations; won all the Battles. She was a Single man Army. As the Balance and Harmony was restored in her Life, she felt keen on writing her Journey.

I strongly feel that the book should reach all those who went through a similar state in Life. They might or might not have overcome the situation. But after reading this book, all of you will surely Feel Empowered and more Strengthened by Life. So allow her to share her life journey with all of you.

It is a personal story where the characters are very much real. She still lives with them, Breathes with them, encounters them everyday. So through this book, she intends to thank all those who became a part of her journey. They Breathes her Growth and added so many colors on the way!

Writing this book has been extremely easy. It seems as if the chapters were Flowing through her like the river that cuts through the mountain and flows from peaks to valleys. She had no apprehension, whatsoever while writing this Book. The best part about sharing your Life Journey with others is that you feel transparent and authentic while delivering the message.

Since the experiences jump directly from her life, you the readers will surely feel the energy and association with your own story.

So relax yourself while reading this book. As you read each chapter, reflect back Into your life and see what did you do when faced with similar situation.

Maybe you responded in a much better way than I did. Maybe you handled the situation better than her. We are not arriving at the conclusion of who did great in Life. Like I mentioned before, each one of us is Unique and we all design our special ways of dealing with situations around. We all strive for the best in life.

And our Happiness always grows deeper when we share the wisdom and success stories in Life.

Finally, when you read this book, you will feel strong, Empowered and more likely Blessed. You will mirror these feelings for others as well. And those others will mirror for some other set of people. It becomes like a ripple effect. Like how Laughter is. Scientists all around have proved that Laughter is contagious.

Similarly, your Positivity, Energy, Spark for life is contagious. It will spread around like wild forest fire. And it will bring you only like minded positive people around.

The purpose of this book is clear. Mona intends to share her process of Growth with everyone around so that they are equally motivated to bring the Transformation in their life. I hope this book fulfils her dream and vision.

Ritambhara
Vedic Tarot Reader & Holistic Healer
www.RitambharaGuides.com

Contents

Foreword   *v*

Preface   *xi*

Introduction   *1*

1. The First Magical Key   7
2. Beauty Inside Out!   13
3. The Beauty Given by Spirituality   21
4. Transformation through a Loss   27
5. Is Your Glass Half Empty or Half Full?   33
6. Don't Try; Just Become   39
7. Music of your Intuition   45
8. Emotional Storms of a Woman   51
9. When You Dream it; You Plan it; You Get It!   57
10. Allow the Universe to Work for You!   61
11. What you Allow is What Will Continue!   67
12. When The Soul Whispers…. Just Listen!   73
13. Find Peace and Freedom in Heart   79
14. Wake Up! Life gives you Multiple Chances…   85

15. Law of Perception	91
16. Giving Birth to a 'Visionary Genius'	97
17. Inner Journey with my Son	101
18. Do Not Discount What a Child Says!	109
19. Closure on the Relationship	113
20. Stand Up and Re-Start your Life!	121
21. Love For Sisters	129
22. Letters to GOD	139
23. Powerful Tool to Achieve your Goals	147
24. Choose Happiness	153
25. Get Money Flowing to you	161
26. Law of Attraction - A blessing in disguise	173
27. The Power of Your Thoughts	181

Introduction

The Book that you are about to read now is going to impact all stages of your Life --- right from the point of Conception To Growth – from Maturity, Decline and Further Rising from your own Ashes (Being a Phoenix).

Mona-Vated is my Initiative to Spread Only One Message across the World ---

Be the Motivation that you always needed in Life.

Just as Rumi says, '*What you seek is seeking you*'.

My Journey revealed the most beautiful yet hidden secrets of Existence. The most important amongst them was --- We can never Motivate Others; Instead We can Only give them the Courage to Motivate Themselves and Stand for their own Truth! As I look back into my Life, I feel Extremely Proud to have deeply inculcated a feeling of Self-Motivation and setting an example for others.

I can just show you the mirror but it is YOU who will have to look inward and create that drive/motivation to move ahead!

This book is a true narration of Mona's Life, her struggles, the drama, the humor, her fall-outs and a new way of Motivation that moved along with every Chapter of her Life. Every single day, I had a new *"Mona-Vated Moment"!!*

I like to call it 'Mona-Vated' as it perfectly synchronizes with the idea of Motivating Self and Living a Powerful Life. Therefore, this book talks about endless 'Mona-Vated Moments' or the 'Eureka or Aha Moments' that occurred during my journey.

It might seem Dramatic, Hilarious, Heart Warming or Philosophical but I promise that towards the end each one of you will look back and count the number of times when you Motivated yourself, feeling that you could have done it better.

If I were to ask you the most fundamental question—Why do we need Motivation in Life?

Most of you will say that Motivation is required to Stay Focused, to stay Strong and to Succeed in Life. That is very true but let me take it a level deeper. The very intrinsic Nature of Human Beings is to move forward. You always want to keep the forward momentum. And when you are constantly doing things to move ahead, you are anyway motivating yourself at every step to go further and further.

The funny thing about taking steps towards your goals is that you eventually get there. The trick is to Motivate yourself and stay in a Positive State about the progress you are making and not to waste time on what is Missing and get deviated from your actual path!

Dear Friends, Brothers, Sisters, I ask you **To Take a Hold of Your Life** because each time you give birth to an Inner Drive, you also create a new Choice of it in Life. You start seeing the Beauty of Life. Look at it with Joy and Smile at it with Sunshine to discover that Sadness will automatically start disappearing. Since Hell and Heaven cannot exist together. You will be left with only one choice.... 'Heaven'!

This book is purely based on my Life Experiences. All the views or statements made around Life are purely Subjective. They are simply my learnings and I do not intend to hurt anyone in the process of narrating these stories. I have gained deep insights during my encounters with my Family and close friends. Even though, we may share a difference in opinions but the ever changing beliefs helped me become a more Empowered Being.

I would specifically like to dedicate this Book to my Mum (who passed away 25 years ago) and to all the Arthritis Patients World-wide. My mother suffered from Arthritis and she had to bear with tremendous pain and suffering from a very early age which I grew up seeing. Later, I did a great amount of research on understanding the core reason for Arthritis. The metaphysical reasons for Arthritis are self-criticism and non-acceptance. It is a disease that comes from constant patterns of criticism. It starts with criticism of self and then criticism of other people. Eventually, people attract a lot more of it into their lives as the pattern imprints.

Negative emotions and lack of self-love cause our Unconscious Mind to purposely induce any diseases in our body. I learned about many such diseases and Arthritis in particular from my personal experiences. I was determined to help those who were willing to grow out of these emotional blockages. A lot of my initial life experiences will talk about my 'Mona-Vated' Moments with my Mother.

I will also like to dedicate this book to my Family, Sisters and all those who crossed my Path as each one of them facilitated my purpose in Life!

P.S. I might ask you to do a Small Exercise in a few Chapters. Each Exercise, if you do it sincerely will enable you to understand the essence of Life, Thoughts, Emotions and how you can Mould yourself in right direction ~

I am dedicating this poem to my Mom and all those kids that have lost their Mother. As much as we have come into peace with our loss but still deep down we feel the missing gaps in our Life.

I also make a humble request to those whose parents are still alive. Express them your Love! Tell them how much you care about them and love them before its too late.

Respect them for who they are! Our parents/our guardians are doing the best they can. Maybe as children we may not feel the intensity of their love but since I am a Mother now; I feel that we are always striving to do best for our child. If we knew any better, we would do it differently.

Start to Accept and Appreciate them for who they are and what they do!

Here is a little poem written by me that I dedicate to my Angel Mother --

I chose to have Happiness in my heart...

Coz you taught me how to put it there..

I believe in being Gentle and compassionate ...

Its because you showed me how to care...

I havo understanding in my thinking ...

Because you shared your wisdom with cheer..

I take every moment as a blessing ..

Because you empowered me to have no fear...

I am courageous enough to stand up for me...

Because i can still feel your strength and i am able to dare ...

Mom where ever you are .. I just want you to know ...

I am Strong and Happy , just dont go on my tears ...

I can still feel you and your guidance around me ...

Because tears help me keep my soul all clear .. .

Thank you mom for all your Love Peace and Blessings.. ..

Because what i learnt from you , is now what I share ....

God really knew how to show himself in physical form ..

That is why he created Moms so his love can be every where ...

May my Mother's soul rest in peace and if it wasn't for my connection with my mom in my mediation; this book probably would have not come into reality. I truly believe loved ones from other side are always supporting in a very unique way

Chapter 1
The First Magical Key
*~ All That I am, or Hope to Be;
I Owe to my Angel Mother ~*

ABRAHAM LINCOLN

I am taking you back to the time when India's Obsession with giving birth to a Male Child had demonstrated serious repercussions on the Society that we lived in. Relationships were tormented and families broken only because the women of family could not produce a male offspring.

Almost 40 years back amidst a time when the society highly valued the birth of a baby boy over that of a girl, my mother gave birth to three beautiful daughters. We were three sisters born in Jalandhar, Punjab. I being the youngest after the birth of two daughters, my family was really looking forward to welcoming a boy in the family at the time of my birth. Thankfully my mother was just happy to welcome her third child to the world and gender didn't seem to matter to her. However, when I came to this world she had to face great deal of resistance from the whole family. Nonetheless, she was determined to save her child from all the societal taboos.

She fought all the stressors and it became clear that ultimately Existence wanted me to follow this path. As a result, I came screaming into the world in the 7th month. Being born in a small town like Jalandhar with almost nil medical facilities and arrangements, doctors had given up on me. They had declared that due to being born as a premature baby, my organs had not fully developed and I would not survive for long. But would that answer ever comfort any mother? She never gave up hope. She use to wrap me in cotton and place me close to 'Angithi' (it is a traditional brazier used for space-heating and cooking mainly in

North India, Pakistan and Nepal. It generates heat from burning coal). She prayed all day long for my survival.

Her prayers were Magic. I survived in spite of all the opposing energies, I also regained my health. As I was growing up, my mother narrated the stories of my magical birth many times and ended it with saying that *'I was here for a special reason'*.

This is my first memory of a 'Mona-Vated Moment'.

"What could be the reason?" I kept asking myself. Why would I fight against all the odds of society and survive? Some meaning, inspiration and contribution started building up as I grew older.

However, a series of not ideal events continued in my family and I wouldn't call them pleasant or fun. My father was working in a different city so he would visit us only 3 or 4 times in a year. My mother started to suffer a lot due to her Arthritis pain and she could barely manage to do the household chores. As a result the three sisters (like the three musketeers) were practically raised by each other. My eldest sister took charge of cooking arena, the middle sister did the household cleaning while the youngest lass (that is me) was appointed with the task of buying grocery. I still remember making my small trips to the Grocery Store to buy soaps, shampoo, snack items.

Each one of us has a very fascinating story from the time we grew up. We all cherish the beautiful moments of playing in the courtyard, visiting neighbors, fighting with each other, or receiving appreciation or a compliment from adults around. Harvard University conducted a Study that says "most of our personality is built by the age of 5". Put in a crude language, "50% of who we are today has been hardwired in our system by the age of 5".

So what does this personality consist of?

It has all your beliefs, thoughts, patterns, conditioning and all this develops from your interaction with your parents, teachers, influential elders and societal norms. At a young age, you are extremely vulnerable. You don't look inside and you don't have the ability to introspect or evaluate. You simply absorb whatever the environment offers you!

So, believe me, the ability to be *Aware* develops much later. But make sure to offer your children an environment that will help them develop a healthy state of mind and body.

I was brought up in an environment that was conducive to my own self-learning. My elder sisters use to make fun of me and tease me by saying that 'I was the unwanted one'. Most of our pranks, conversation or tiny fights would end up in these comments. However, what seemed like a joke would shrink me into a shell inside. I was locking myself inside a cage that was built on a 'Need for Acceptance' and 'Need for Love'. But understand one thing, when we close ourselves from hurt, we miss out on Life. As we also close ourselves from receiving Love, Support and Beauty.

Even a small emotion has the ability to lead a chain-reaction! My Grades started falling and I stopped speaking to other people or being involved. When we would have family, friends, guests come over our place; everyone would chat and interact with each other except me who would sit for hours without saying a single word. My mother would continuously sarcastically question her youngest daughter was deaf and dumb.

But the little girl deep inside cried uncontrollably, and said that she did not want to be heard or seen because of her extreme low self-esteem.

Days passed without much change happening inside-out. I eventually entered the college. It was a Girl's College and my low profile would make me silently disappear in the crowd. However through one of the college festivals, a friend suggested that I should participate in the college fashion show. The mere thought of participation seemed crazy, deceiving and defying to my personality. My inner conscience would never allow me to walk the ramp.

How Could I ever be Accepted?

Why will People Appreciate Me?

Why should I walk the ramp when I know that no one will acknowledge?

They might make fun of me... a tornado of negative statements revolved around my mind. A part of me was willing to participate while the other part crossed fired and reminded me of all my hurtful childhood stories. Finally, the *'Mona-Vated Moment'* arrived. Just a day before, I gave my name and decided to walk the ramp! (To explore more about myself)

Without deciding on costumes and with zero practice, I made an Inner Statement.

I am going to do this anyhow!

Finally, I did. I walked the ramp. And I smiled all along. Faces glanced at me and I walked with all my Grace. I didn't care to win the contest because I had already Won the Contest inside. To my surprise, I made it to the list of top 6 runners' up.

That is the day when my inner Goddess had come into power. The feeling of belonging had returned. It seemed as if I was re-born with hundreds of arms welcoming me!

All I knew was that--- One Decision--- to be part of Competition had given me another life, another chance to live with Glory!

Life is continuously offering us Glorious Moments. It is 'US' who needs to pay a closer look. Even a slightest change to your Daily Schedule can add so much Richness to your Life!

Chapter 2
Beauty Inside Out!

Let me first ask you ---

"What does it mean to be open?"

Does it mean to accept Life without judgment? Or to feel happy no matter what comes? Is it to criticize less, accept others more and learn more about their wonderful aspects?

It simply means experiencing Life fully!

But does that happen instantly?

Can you wake up one morning and say that 'From today onwards, I am going to be open to Life; I will not judge myself or others; I will not expect anything and I will not get upset, irritated or frustrated even if things aren't as I'd like them to be.

The truth is that we are in a Dynamic Environment and we are constantly surrounded by emotions, feelings and thoughts. No matter how much we like it or we don't, we are constantly bombarded with environmental stimuli. So I have always believed in Steady Growth. I have always seen Life as a Continuous Learning Process. It might seem like a slow process but in many small ways I've learnt a lot, and I am much more open now than I have ever been before.

I'll share one of my experiences of 'being open to life', in hope that you'll find your 'MonaVated Moment' too after reading this—

One of the prejudices that have remained for very long in the Indian Society was the 'preference for fair-skin girls'. People's obsession with fair skin has led many young women to the brink of suicide. Being fair was synonymous with being beautiful while having a dusky or wheatish skin color was considered to be average or underrated looks!

Can you imagine how it shakes the confidence of a young girl who has not even explored the secrets of her own body?

It is like placing a horrible burden on yourself. Every time, you see your reflection in the mirror, it reflects shame or trauma. Women take drastic measures to conceal this pain.

Being part of a small town, we were always surrounded by the age old customs and stereotypes. Here as well, the connotation of 'Beauty' was directly proportionate to skin color, specifically for the girls in our community. My mother and my elder sisters were blessed with fair skin. However, I was blessed with a dusky complexion. I was made to realize the significance of fair skin at very young age. Being called as 'Kali' (hindi name for black color) wasn't a pleasant experience as I mentally segregated myself and shifted into a different compartment.

"I was not the same as others and I am not appreciated as I am."

As a young girl and a teenager, I allowed these remarks to hurt me deeply. I was very shy already and this made me even more self-conscious as I was constantly aware of people speaking about me.

I was reserved and in my shell which led me to hiding most of the time. At the age of 19, I was sent to Canada as my elder sister was settled there and was sponsoring me. I had never found the acceptance to my skin color but life just moved on for me like an average girl who goes to work in the morning and comes back home in evening with no zest or passions.

One of those days as I walked back home from work, I saw a board that read, 'Tanning Salon'.

Amusing!

I had heard about Beauty Salon, Hair Salon, Nail Salon….

What do they mean by 'Tanning Salon'?

My inquisitiveness drove me inside. A lady attended to me as I entered. I was keen so I jumped straight to the point.

"Forgive me, I am new to this town, can you please tell me what do you mean by tanning salon? I have never heard about this before".

Well, this is the place where we help people get tanned. There are a lot of people who pay to get tanned during the summers here. As I looked around with awe and wonderment, the women replied,

You wouldn't require this Dear;

You already have the perfect skin color;

In fact people would die to get that skin color!

Her voice was no more heard! Time froze immediately. It seemed as if the world had come to a halt. I had no clue how I reached home that day! The moment I entered the house, I rushed into the bathroom. My father saw me dazed and asked whether I was fine. To which I replied, that 'I needed to freshen up'. Almost for 30 minutes in washroom, I stood in front of the mirror and stared at myself.

All this apprehension around my skin color; my low self-esteem; was not required at all, I told myself!

My Mona-Vated Moment came out loud and clear!

I saw myself in new light.

I am no longer going to beat myself about it; I no longer feel nervous about it!

What was once my biggest weakness had now transformed to my biggest strength!

All these years, I felt miserable about my skin-color, I felt underprivileged. Whereas I realized that the world (that exists beyond me) sees it as Blessing. That day, I promised that I would care for myself. I promised to get up each day and see myself in the mirror to feel more and more loved. At a time when I knew nothing about affirmations my inner strength grew by leaps and bounds as I did this little exercise each morning!

Next day, I walked like a Lady. The poise and elegance of a princess had returned from the hidden realm. I could regain the innocence of young pretty Mona who dressed up and felt beautiful about herself.

To my surprise, I had appreciation and compliments showering on me like dew drops. While I stood on the sky train station waiting to board the train to my work, a lady walks up to me to say, 'I have never seen a more beautiful women'. You have such a pretty face, any color would suit you'.

From strangers, to known people, to colleagues, to my clients, people randomly walked over to appreciate my looks. Today, when I look back, I know this was my biggest break-through!

The most powerful 'Mona-Vated Moment'…

My Inner World created the Outer World. This experience let me uncover the biggest secret

~~~ It is all created by you ~~~

The way we feel within our body affects not only us but the world beyond; so the moment I changed the reflection within me; I saw a magnificent change in the outer world. It might have taken me years to discover this Principle. But like I said, the process can be slow but it will surely facilitate you in 'Being open to Life' and master the Art of Inner and Outer Harmony!

Chapter 3
The Beauty Given by Spirituality

My Journey with Spirituality is beyond my comprehension. Sometimes you feel like there are no reasons for why certain things happen to you in Life! It is best not to give them any reason or meaning.

I was still naive. Innocence covered me in a beautiful shield. I was hardly 3 year old when my journey with spirituality began! Since I lived in a small town, more like a village; we had the habit of getting up early. All year round, I got up early, took bath with cold water and walked towards the nearest temple which had a beautiful Shivlinga. I poured water over the Shivlinga (ritual of pouring the water over Shivlinga signifies that we calming the internal fire and channelizing Life Force Energy).

Then I would walk towards the church where I lit candles before Christ, my next destination would be the mosque and finally the gurudwara where the Ardas (morning prayer) and kirtan would lit up my eyes and body with happiness!

Finally, I would walk towards my school. I would start early every morning so that I could visit all these places before reaching school.

Why would I feel inclined to visit all these places?

What would I ask from God?

As a little girl, I did not have any complications or big visions in Life. There was no desire as such except for little goodies which I anyway got from my elders around!

I visited those places because I felt more beautiful and cheerful when being around these Sacred and Holy places.

It would seem surprising how a little girl would feel happy playing in and around the Temples, Gurudwaras or Churches all alone instead of being around with her peer group!

Have you ever heard that when someone doesn't find Beauty within, he looks for Beauty outside? He tries to beautify everything around only to fill up the emptiness inside!

As a young girl, I was given a name. A name which stayed with me for many years and shattered my beliefs about myself! I was called 'kali' (Hindi name for Black color) simply because I had a dusky skin tone. I was not fair and thus beautiful as per Indian Standards!

And as mentioned before, since I was an unwanted child, there were many reasons to be disrespectful and less loving towards me.

I was a young mind, vulnerable to all the inputs. At that age, we do not select or introspect the information that we receive; we just absorb whatever is coming to us. So I am left standing with a wall around me. Deep inside me, I did not feel good and felt like I was a topic of everyone's giggles or even an embarrassment for my mother.

Various relatives and friends would come together and call out my name. That wasn't pleasing at all and the feeling of being mocked or being unacceptable was growing within me. I didn't know what to do with it until I started to visit all these holy places.

There you go! Eureka! I found my home!

Now, I am at the place where I feel Beautiful, I feel deeply relaxed even when I am alone. I knew that I was fully accepted and appreciated here!

The Energy of all the Holy Places and Sacred Chanting uplifted my spirit. I felt so playful. The sheer Innocence of me as a child returned. I would play around these worship areas. It seemed as if I was given the most comfortable environment to grow and explore myself.

Today, as I look back, I feel the connection with Spirituality helped me release my emotions even when I did not know what Emotions meant to me!

A lot of people believe that Spirituality makes you serious in Life. It makes you detached from worldly affairs. But for me, the idea of Spirituality was simple. It was something that helped me outgrow a feeling/belief that would have otherwise destroyed me completely.

Chapter 4
Transformation through a Loss
~ Don't Grieve. Anything you lose comes round in another form ~

RUMI

I am merely 16 years old, studying in X Grade. On 15th August, my mother fell very ill. Since we were residing in Jalandhar, from there we took her to Beas, which was the neighborhood town and obviously, next best place for Medical facilities. I clearly remember 5 people in the car. The front seats were occupied by driver and my paternal uncle while the back seats were occupied by me, my sister and my mother lying with her head on my sister's lap and her feet on my lap.

As we reached the Beas Hospitals, we were informed that she would require Dialysis which was only available in Chandigarh Hospitals. So we drove from Beas to Chandigarh in search of comfort for my mum. On entering, she was immediately addressed by a set of Doctors. I remember seeing her in that Emergency Ward, it was the last eye contact that we had. She seemed to be in real pain but at the same time, she was not willing to leave her body; to take the final journey towards freedom.

My sisters and me were sent out of the ward as the doctors wanted to examine her extensively. It wasn't until then that she gave away and a few minutes later we got to know that she passed away.

~ Life is very precarious, accidental, at any moment anybody can go;

And eventually we are all here to Disappear sooner or later ~

OSHO

But the reality at that time seemed very hard. It seemed as if thousand lifetimes were taken away from me at that moment. When someone comes across grief and loss, they never look into the explanations and consolations; instead we just look at the Naked Truth. And the truth is that my mother was no more alive! I was too young to comprehend the deeper meanings of Life and Death so I never went on to asking 'Why me', 'Why my mother', 'What for'…

All I knew was that I was in a shock and was broken into a thousand pieces. All I can remember Now is the pain, hurt and sadness as we carried her back home; just in the same manner as we brought her to the hospital. Even while going back, she was lying on the back seat with her head on my sister's lap and her feet on my lap.

Somehow the thinking stopped. The shock was such that the mind was blurred. And the only feeling that hit me instantly was

"Why were we not with her while she was going away?"

"Why did she have to go away after we came out of the ward?"

"Why didn't she say a goodbye to us before going away?"

The questions kept pondering in my Mind even after completing all the rituals. The funny thing about Life is --- Everything fades away with time whether it is plants, trees, flowers, fruits, animals, rocks, humans and even their memories.

Time Heals Everything!

We had to finally return to the normal functioning, return to schools, prepare food at home and do the same chores as we did before. The only difference was --- we could not see our mother in the drawing room, resting in the bedroom nor having food with us.

Like I mentioned earlier, those three questioned kept rotating in my mind and the pain in my heart had now become unbearable.

It had to be left for the new. It had to go away as the new mind was waiting to give way to 'Mona-Vated Moments'. Each transformation is a painful process. It is not easy. It is not always pleasant. It requires you to move from what is familiar, known and secure (old patterns) and replace it with new, absolutely unknown patterns or thoughts. Simply put, it follows the principles of your physical body. Every moment many cells in your body are dying and many new ones are being reborn. Physiologists say that the body is a "flux", river like. So when the old cells die, the new ones take their place. Same happens with your mind.

When something goes missing; something new enters its place!

My Mona-Vated Moment arrived and I finally realized that your beloved person never wants YOU to see them dying. When the time comes to die, the heart is filled with fear. It is not about losing an individual; it is more about losing a hope in someone's eyes. Till the last moment, humans do not Drop the Bondage of Hope! Unless you are totally destroyed in the Mind, there is always Hope for you.

We will always keep trying; we will always keep hoping that it gets better. HOPE is a Universal feeling. It is always the same everywhere. A feeling that keeps you alive, motivated and makes you travel the road to Victory. We had hoped for a better and healthy future for our mother but when it reached the dead end; my mother made sure that we turn our heads back so that we look at the wide road ahead. She wanted us to **keep the Faith and the Attitude of moving ahead; instead of seeing it as an End.**

My understanding of Soul's Purpose came much later but what I arrived at in the beginning was the profound understanding of human life and the very purpose of survival.

Today as I look back, I feel immensely touched and moved while thinking of those little precious moments spent with my mother. From the age of three, I saw her limping and unhealthy but even after being in a state of discomfort she showed me a reflection of Life.

The Journey of a Human Being is only about attaining a Balanced State of Mind & Balanced State of Body!

The Higher Soul purpose can wait for longer but first begin your Journey towards a Healthy and Harmonious Body!

Chapter 5
Is Your Glass Half Empty or Half Full?

~ Don't dwell on what went wrong. Instead, focus on what to do next. Spend your energies on moving forward toward finding the answer ~

DENIS WAITLEY

Amongst the three of us, my eldest sister got married while the other one was still in college. I was still trying to cope with studies (X Standard) and my mother's demise together. Just as I was in the process of recovering from my grief and loss, I was asked to pack my bags and move to Canada.

My middle sister got married in Canada and eventually got her sponsorship as well; while the elder one was already settled there with her family. Since I was young, they did not want to leave me behind. In spite of zero motivation, I was somehow convinced to move from my base. I was not keen on leaving my country as I always had this deep connection with my land, my belongingness and culture. I thought to myself, 'it might be a great place to live but I am not going out of my own willingness.' When circumstances force you to make a decision, you are compelled to act. You are forced to make a decision. The only helpful tool at that moment is -

> *Follow the Instructions of Universe and flow with it. Accept whatever comes your way because when you try to resist, it causes more Pain and Troubles.*

To keep my father happy, I moved to Canada. Since, we had just moved to the country, it took him some time before he got a job. Days were passing by and there was no source of income which started creating apprehensions within us. As a result, I decided to take up a part time job. Since I was young and an enthusiast learner, I was pretty sure that I would get a job faster and more easily. I started working in a retail store. Time passed by so fast. I felt like an Hourglass, the sand moved from one glass bulb to another. And before I realized, I had stepped into a new dimension of life. I was now a fully fledged working woman.

I realized that I was the only bread-earner of the family so I did not have much of an option except to continue working. The three years of working experience was phenomenal. The Money that I received took care of me and my father's needs. We were grateful to Life as we were blessed with good health, food and some generous moments of love that.

Gratitude unlocks the fullness of life!

With sheer Gratitude, your denial will turn into acceptance; chaos turns into order and vacuum will be replaced by fullness and abundance. We were making all our minutes with significant efforts to turn our life around. Everything around us was helping us dissolve the emotional pain that we had undergone as a family. As a result, our spirits felt alive. Over the years I realized that living a simple and healthy life is a great boon! I was being offered great learnings at my work place and it now seemed appropriate to say that I was being born again. It seemed like a flower was being born out of a crisis!

My job helped me understand the corporate dimension very well. Every part of my personality was polished for bigger and better work in Life!

I knew I was going through a Transition. But the circumstances had also triggered a feeling of helplessness. My desire to study was buried deep inside. All these life situations asked me to keep moving ahead but also pushed my basic desires (desire to study further) beneath the carpet. I denied myself of the education in order to resolve the ongoing challenges.

Many a times, we cry out to God or Universe… *this is the Desire of my heart!*

One such desire of my heart was to study further and go deeper into my field of interest. However, our feelings and mind take us on different roads of Life and as Humans we are bent out of circumstances. The best that you can do in such a time is –

Truly hear what Existence is trying to convey to you!

You might feel frustrated; you might even feel deceived simply because you are turning deaf and blind towards your own feelings. Here is when the Mona-Vated Moment arrived ---

I could have chosen to see the Glass as half empty or half full!

There are many stories around it and I like to raise this question many a times in order to see how I perceive events and objects in my life.

Is the glass half empty or half full?

Half a glass of water is kept on the table. When I pick up the same glass and ask you "is the glass half empty or half full?" Your answer to this simple question will reveal a lot about individual traits and your world views. You could either see it as half full (optimism) or half empty (pessimism).

At that moment, I chose to see my **Glass as Half Full.** I might have had to shed my dreams (of studying further) but I was surely making the best out of the present situation.

The SECRET to LIFE is --- DEVELOPING AN ATTITUDE!

An attitude where you make the best out of any situation that is being offered to you. It is very easy for all of us to just label the situation as 'Bad' or 'Good'. When we see the situation as 'Bad', we take a back seat and blame it on circumstances whereas when we see the situation as 'Good', we take a plunge and feel happy because everything is favorable.

But the Real Story of Life is only revealed when you keep moving ahead without labeling any Event/Situation and do the best in every event of Life.

Chapter 6
Don't Try; Just Become
*~ The Journey of a thousand miles
begins with one Step ~*
Lao - Tzu

Experience Life in all possible ways – good-bad; bitter-sweet; dark-light; summer-winter....

In the Last Chapter, we spoke about a woman's effort to make the Best of Life. In this chapter, I am specifically going to take you along to see **how the path was created when I started walking on it**. Our understanding of Life is too frivolous at times. Lack of Certainty makes the Human Mind so apprehensive that we feel like we can walk the path only when it is properly lit and the directions are laid down precisely.

Whereas, Life will always show you another way around. You will be asked to walk and as you are walking, you are going to get a better clarity of where you are heading! Let me explain this with a small example. When I was a little kid, I visited one of the Grocery stores with my elder sister. Few days later, I was supposed to buy couple of things from the same grocery store. But this time, I was not accompanied by my sister. So I had to figure out the way to the store all by myself. I started walking, a little fearful and a little confused but as I moved ahead, I remembered the way! I was able to create a mental image of the same road and the next few turns. Finally I reached the store. With great Enthusiasm in my heart, I felt confident and proud of myself. Even though I was perplexed at the start of my journey, I reached where I had to.

Finally, all our efforts are towards making this Life more meaningful!

Coming back to my journey, I had taken certain drastic decisions of Life after moving to Canada. One of them was jumping into the work front with a Big Leap of Faith. I was completely alien to the city. But as I moved ahead to Explore the city; it lead to a deeper exploration of myself. Being able to interact with people from different cultures and different backgrounds of the society helped me evolve as a more Conscious and Social Being. Surprisingly, I was offered two promotions in the same company.

Dreams may not Manifest in Life (the way the dreamer wants) but he must wait until the Life gives him a Gift that seem better than the Dream! The Beautiful Land of Canada gave me tons of opportunity for Growth, Upliftment, and Confidence building. It helped me reveal the Latent Energy and Passion towards my Work.

As I stepped out, I got a job within one month of look through. My first work place was far from where I stayed. There was no proper transit system to work so I had to take 4 buses and one sky train to reach my workplace. Sometimes, I used to come back at 2 am and had to hurry up the next morning for opening the store again at 8 am; which precisely meant that I had to get up at 5 am in morning.

Commuting can have serious impact on mental and physical health. I was tired by the untimely sleeping and waking up patterns. I felt very fatigued and drained, but I could never gather the Courage to speak to my company regarding it. I was submissive to the whole situation as I knew the importance of my first Job and money that I brought home. Later, I came to know that the company had other branches as well and I could ask for a Transfer to a Branch that was pretty close to my home. However, the very thought of losing the job was scary due to which I was giving in whatever it required.

This is where we need to evaluate that whatever we do in life --- Is it out of Compulsion or Independence?

Although, I was not working with the feeling of Freedom, but I guess this is where time was testing my real Inner Strength. I explored all the dimensions of my work profile and later undertook the tasks that went beyond my profile duties. As a result, I was promoted to be a Store Lead by the 2nd month and in another 8 months; I was made the Head of Department.

Just like a whirlpool, I kept wandering from one direction to another. My success stories had not ended here. Within one year, I was appointed as the Manager of Department and the next three years finally got me up to the level of an Operations Manager!

If I were to look deeper into my success stories, I would feel Joyful, Proud, Peaceful and Accepted within myself.

Each Step was bringing New Discoveries so I do not have any particular 'Mona-Vated Moment' to share here. But I will surely share my constant feelings of Frenzy and Bliss as I expanded my outer Knowledge and also worked through my Inner Wisdom.

I was not running for my final Destination or Goal. Instead I knew that I was here only to enjoy my Journey. The road that I was traveling was more important than reaching a place and ending it all.

Chapter 7
Music of your Intuition

*~ Wearing a mask wears you out. Faking it is Fatiguing.
The most Exhausting Activity is pretending to
be what you know you aren't ~*

RICK WARREN

I migrated to Canada in the year 1993. I was 19 year old when I came to this Magical Land.

I was young, naïve and still unprepared to see the world in its full glory. Coming from a small town in India, I had seen a very different facet of society, environment and relationships. Whereas when I moved to Canada, I was in complete awe and surprise of the culture, the people and their lifestyles. Honestly, it took me a while to cope with the surrounding. It did not seem hard but I was surely taking time to accept the newer dimensions of work, relating to people and living a balanced life.

When I turned 22, my father came forward to tell me the hardest truth of Life. He said, *"you must get married now; Are you seeing someone?"*

Seeing someone?

That sounded like the strangest thing to me. There were not many friends, not many associations so I had absolutely no scope and opportunity to invite anyone in my life. As I denied that vital question, my father continued with his authority, "in that case, we shall find a suitable boy for your marriage".

Parents finding a suitable boy for their daughters may be unheard and unseen thing in many countries. But it is part of the rich cultural heritage in India. We belonged to a society where the Daughters were seen as a responsibility for the parents and being married by the age of 22 or 23 was the most appropriate thing to do. This would ensure a smooth running of families. My father was considerate enough to ask me if I had a liking towards anyone. In most cases, the parents would never ask their daughters. The decision was completely onto them. The scenarios may have changed now in India but the idea of arrange marriage still prevails in the Indian society.

Before I could blink my eyes, my father had put up my advertisement on Indian Matrimony. This simply means that my profile will be shared with all the other potential candidates. Soon, we received tons of responses. It is funny to see how one event leads to another. At that moment, I was in no state to think or introspect. I was moving with the flowing wind!

However, it was strange how I could make firm decisions at work while I was unable to take any decision at personal front. Sometimes, we come across situations where our decisions lead to better results. This makes us extremely confident of ourselves. But we forget that Life keeps giving us challenges. And every decision that you take may not lead you to better results. So the best is to uncover new facets at all point in life. It helps us to grow and find a unique way of resolution each time.

My story continued as each day brought new marriage proposals from India. My Dad and my Sisters finished shortlisting amongst the list of candidates. And the final picture was shown to me. I was asked to go to India to meet the boy and his family. So I took leave and undertook my journey to India. I was not accompanied by anyone from the family, neither my father or my sisters nor my step mum who was in India. I was just supposed to stay at my sister's friend's place.

Next day, we waited for the boy and his family to arrive. These were the days when residing in Canada (or anywhere overseas) was a big status symbol. So many young boys and girls looked forward to marry partners who were already established in other countries.

As I am waiting for the family to arrive, I had an intense feeling. It seemed as if my Instinct screamed to me and said a 'No' to this marriage proposal.

Suddenly, I had clarity over the whole situation. I was sure that I did not want to invite this energy into my life. However, it was not an appropriate time to jump and cry out loud.

Trust the small voice inside you; which tells you exactly what to say; what to decide!

During those days, the girl and boy were left alone for 5 minutes to talk and make a decision about the biggest event of their life! After few minutes, his father came close to me and asked 'how was our conversation?'

I gently replied that it was a good conversation. The next moment, I see everyone congratulating, celebrating and joyfully smiling as they saw a perfect matrimony alliance. Thereafter, I was not allowed to say even the next sentence.

After two days, I saw myself engaged to the guy who I spoke for 5 minutes. We met a couple of times over lunches and dinners before I left for Canada. Most of the women from India might relate with this story. It may not happen in a similar manner now but most of the arrange marriage setups are done in a similar manner.

When I reached back home, my father asked me again whether I was happy with my decision. I said 'Yes'.

The Most Confused we ever get is when we try to convince our heads of something our hearts know is a lie ~~

Karen Moning

I could not gather the courage to tell the truth to my father. Somewhere, I felt that he was under societal obligation and great pressure to get me married. I did not want to add to his stress.

Today, as I revive those moments, I would know that I did not do any good to my father or me.

Your Beliefs don't make you a better person; your Behavior does…

Towards the end, I knew that my beliefs and behavior did not synchronize. What I did was actually against my own thoughts/beliefs. So I had to face the consequences as well. After 7 months, he got his sponsorship and after 5 days of him moving to the country, we got married.

Chapter 8
Emotional Storms of a Woman

Marriage to me was beyond the paper. It was more about 'the meeting of two souls' and bringing love, respect, understanding and faith to the partnership!

Like any other young girl, I was excited and romanticizing about my honeymoon. I took 2 weeks off and we went for our honeymoon. Little did I know that we would spend those days traveling from one University to another, just to evaluate his certificates? I use to dress-up and feel excited about each day and deeper exploration of one another. But to my surprise, the whole agenda of the trip was something else. Rest of the time was spent in the hotel room as he insisted that we save most of the money!

The Money that he brought along was deposited as a Fixed Deposit. So I was taking care of all the expenses during that time. Two entire weeks but there was no soul connection.

The most vital thing to understand about **soul connection** is --- it is not some incarnation or meta-physical concept. It simply means that two people are drawn towards each other because there is an inner feeling of belongingness. This feeling itself is so powerful that it does not require any language or words.

Later my married life was put into the same frame as it was for my mother. I would get up early morning to prepare his meals; carry out the household chores and also continue with my job as I was taking care of all bills and lifestyle. He started doing some odd jobs whereas I was settled with a steady job. So I was making sure to give my 100% to this relationship and new beginning.

I referred him to various places but he could not sustain in any job for more than 3 days. He kept shuffling jobs for a year until I made him realize one day that the work culture is very different between Canada and India. Coming from an Indian background and culture, he was used to a particular set of tasks and lot of leniency being offered whereas working in Canada means that you have to understand Ethics, time at work and growth prospects.

The next two years were very challenging.

I conceived and was carrying a child while I was working and serving him with humility and graciousness. He would require his food on time (at least a 3 course meals) irrespective of whether I was late from work or feeling sick (morning sickness, nausea experienced during pregnancy).

> *Being supportive in your marriage isn't always so well defined but your actions and attitude defines your Love and Understanding towards the Relationship!*

It was the Karva-Chauth night (one day festival celebrated by Hindu women in North India in which married women fast from sunrise to moonrise and pray for the safety and longevity of their husbands). Since I was fasting the entire day, I relaxed and got a little late for evening dinner. Delay in serving dinner lead to a chaos, arguments through which he pushed me off the couch even though I was carrying his child.

This was the last straw that broke the camel's back. Things had gone much beyond my threshold. After 2 years, I called my family to seek their support in these crucial moments.

My family intervened and their support brought me some relief.

But I eventually understood that his behavior and attitude was the result of his upbringing and certain thoughts that are conditioned in an Indian boy at very early age. For example, most of Indian men are very controlling. So was he. Women in families can't make any purchases on their own. It is entirely a man's decision of what to buy and where to buy from? His mother was treated in the similar manner therefore; he made sure that I was following the same track!

My whole pursuit to understand him and his life lead me to become more and more submissive. I thought I needed to adapt. I forgot that the very essence of Love and Relationship is based on establishing Harmony with someone. And how would the harmony persist when we see ignorance, control and domination. Love is Authentic only when it gives Freedom; when it respects the other person's individuality, his or her privacy!

> *Nobody else can destroy you except you;*
> *nobody else can save you except you!*
>
> *You are the Judas and you are Jesus!*
>
> *Osho*

This reminds me of a little story that will make you understand how we give our remote control to others and let them run our life!

One of the days, when I come back home from Shopping; I realize that the door to my main gate is open. Terrified and all apprehensive, I quickly enter the home thinking that maybe I was robbed!

As I enter my home, I see my friend sitting comfortably in the drawing room and watching television. Seeing her, I felt at ease. However, she was roaming freely in my home, watching the television, using the kitchen and other utilities. Since, she was the one who designed the house; she kept cribbing about the paintings not being placed in the right direction and the rooms being untidy.

She used to sit on my favorite chair, eats the goodies that I saved for my evening and complains about the room while watching my favorite show!

What kind of feelings do you think will this experience invoke in me?

I was bound to get agitated, furious and upset about her behavior!

Now, if I had to ask all of you, what lead to this situation; what would you say?

Most of you will say that since she is a friend and also designed your home, she ought to behave authoritatively! But if I don't appreciate such behavior, what do you think I should do?

I simply need to take the remote control back into my hands.

Till this moment, I had given my remote control to someone else and let them run any channel they like. But now, it was time to take the authority back into your hands.

Understanding the other person is very important but more importantly, we need to understand ourselves. Time passed and I was emptied of any emotions or love. I had stopped responding to my own feelings. I sometimes brought him presents but he would make me return them back to the stores because he saw it as money wastage. So I stopped buying or doing anything for him.

Deep down, I was shutting myself as I was denied Love!

Sitting and Introspecting, I questioned myself ---

Is there a difference between *'Denying the Love from others'* and

'Denying the Love from yourself'??

There my Mona-Vated Moment Arrived!

Chapter 9
When You Dream it; You Plan it; You Get It!

We bought a house while I was still pregnant. I was seven months pregnant when I heard the news that my husband was laid off from work.

I was stunned, angry and abandoned. The feelings were strong as I felt highly pressurized towards life! I had to work full time now and take care of all the payments. Meanwhile, my son was born.

> *There is an Immense Happiness while bringing a new soul into the world.*

> *Conception, pregnancy, child birth are very important events of Life. Once it happens, your journey never remains the same. You need to Nourish, Nurture and Protect the new being!*

I was working very hard to give all the support and comforts to my child. We had bought a new house while I was still pregnant. I desired that my child should be born in our new home so I made sure to create this reality. When my son turned 2 year old, my husband made the decision of doing a short IT course. It involved full time study which means that he would not be able to take up any job during that period. I was well aware of the fact that all the household bills and child's expenses would be my responsibility thereafter!

Embarking on this fascinating journey, I agreed and supported his desire. He was passionate about taking up a better and higher paying job after completing the course. I did not want to interfere in his dreams and his journey to success. Instead, I did everything to support him on the way!

As my husband enrolled for the course, I quit my high flying job in retail and instead took a job of an administration assistant. The previous job allowed me only enough time to see my son and work at one place. Whereas the new job kept me engaged from 9am to 5pm. Later in evening, I worked as a waitress in restaurant (Thursday, Friday Evenings). Working all day long on Saturday and Sunday made sure that I generated that extra bit to meet our growing expenses.

However, in this whole arrangement, I had only three evenings in a week where I dedicate the time to my son! Rest of his time was spent in the day care centre. The work schedule just allowed me 30 minutes of free time in between while I got ready for my next shift in the evening. In these 30 minutes, I was supposed to finish household chores and also spend some loving moments to my son!

This went on for seven months. I could make money and also save enough to buy a brand new car for ourselves. My husband looked surprised and shocked when I broke this news to him. He could not believe that I had managed the expenses and also saved enough for the car I had always desired!

You have the Power to manifest anything your Heart Desires.

I focused on my Desire &

What I got is simply the Result of the Energy I gave out!

Chapter 10
Allow the Universe to Work for You!
Life begins where fear ends.

When your soul begins to answer; you will move from 'being unfulfilled' to 'being completely free and fulfilled.

Our Life was moving at such a fast pace that it seems to pass us by before we could really enjoy! My husband had finished his course but he never got a stable job. Any job that he got into was very short lived. As a result, expenses were more or less taken care by me.

When my son was one month old, I had a vivid dream which later became my heartfelt desire that my son should study in India for at least 2 years and be well acquainted with our cultural heritage, our roots, our foundation and sing our National Anthem someday!

But like any other desire, it came to me as fleeting moments and drifted away the next minute.

As my son grew, I established my own business. One of the major reasons for doing so was to pull out more time for my son. With my current job, I was unable to spend enough quality time with my son. He had already turned 5 and majorly grew up at day care center. My long hours of working made me feel guilty for not being able to contribute to his upbringing. I was in a management position with a great company. I felt fulfilled as a working women but at the same time, I felt inadequate as a mother!

After 2 weeks of him turning five, I put down my papers to the organization. I did not know what I will do next. How will I reimburse this source of income? What exactly will I start up?

Without finding answers to any of these questions, I just took a call of life. Left my job truly believing that Existence will find me a way!

~ Look at the sky. We are not alone. The whole universe is friendly to us and conspires only to give the best to those who dream and work ~

A.P.J Abdul Kalam

My dream **Now** was to pick up my boy from school; listen to the countless stories that he brings back home and watch him take every step towards learning and growth. I had seen a childhood where my mother was ill while my father was out of town. Isolation during childhood is detrimental to child's social development and I wanted to make sure that my son never goes through the same.

Surprisingly, as I started with my own business, I was making more money with fewer hours. This led to more beautiful moments being spent with my son. Soon I realized that your desires are in perfect rapport with how the universe works!

Only if you allow, the Universe will work in the perfect way that it knows...

Sometimes you don't have to see the whole of staircase, just see the next step as you move ahead one at a time. I took a big leap, maybe a risky step but I chose to trust the Existence and its workings. I started minting Money. I had my own branch and many people working for me. Eventually, I made a home, I brought my dream car. In short, all the material and physical goods such as money, luxury items that could make any human being happy was present around! Subsequently, I was satisfied with the entire environment that I had created for myself and my family.

Here I will ask all of you to do an **Exercise**—

Sit in an enclosed, silent space. Try and remove all the external stimuli or surrounding sounds. Now close your eyes, take few deep breaths. Hold on to that stillness and ask yourself:

Do I feel good with my present Life?

This might seem like a simple or mundane exercise but your answer will release a lot of energies and emotions in the Body. This thought provoking question will help you Discover that which needs to be addressed urgently.

We are simply Emotional Beings who keep pursuing our heart's desires till the end. But the real Discovery takes place when you come to know -- *"What do I actually Desire?"*

When you bring your full attention to the emotion you are feeling in a certain moment, you will feel something being released. Either it is a new revelation or a thought or a decision that has been waiting for long in your life.

After this exercise, my eyes opened a new dimension within—

I experience an Intense Feeling of Emptiness within me!

I had done everything to make myself happy. Felt empowered when my son was awarded 'The Top Entrepreneur' at school. But deep down, I experienced loss of energy and scarcity of Love. The love from my partner was always missing. And though, I had channelized my energy in various directions, I came back home to feel the same emptiness.

When we feel the profoundness of a relationship, specifically, a sacred bond of Marriage, there is a lot more than just Physical relationship. There is depth of emotions and belongingness that comes along when you share the same bed! However, my marriage was just restricted to physical proximity! Every evening, I would go back to the bed to experience the same kind of routine. Making Love without feeling the real love between us and then sleeping in hope to experience a better, fulfilling day tomorrow.

On one of those nights, when we got over with our routine practice, I came out running towards the stairs while my husband was sleeping away to glory. It was 2 am in morning; I sat on my staircase and began to sob. Eventually, I cried out loud. The dam finally broke and tears flooded out of my eyes and my stomach. It seemed as if something was piercing my gut!

I cried after 10 years and I let it all out.

Is this worth it?

Why am I in it when I don't feel anything in this relationship?

Those two questions changed my life. That moment turned everything as I started re-evaluating my Life!

When the Soul starts to answer, the Universe just makes the changes accordingly!

Within next 2 months, my husband left for India to close a business deal!

Chapter 11
What you Allow is What Will Continue!

Like any other expected and surprising ventures, my husband had come up with a new idea. He had decided on starting a new business in partnership with someone in India. My husband had been speaking very highly of India. He considered India as a goldmine and called it 'the land of opportunities'. I was not convinced on the business proposal and even the partnership but he had made his mind and asked us to just follow. Inside my heart, I knew it was a tough decision. My father, sisters, everyone close to me was settled in Canada. My son was well established with his studies and curriculum here. Leaving all of it behind and re-establishing in India was not an easy call. Yet, I again supported his new venture in lieu of his passion and enthusiasm to move ahead in Life.

Within next 3 months, we packed our bags and came to India looking for great opportunities that this country had to offer. It was difficult to convince my son as he was not keen on moving to new school and a new environment. As we reached India, I kept my eyes open to this new venture and reminded my husband of all the advantages and shortcomings of running the Business. I asked him to participate in the whole working and affairs. Being involved would have given us a better picture of the Business. But he would mostly sit at home as the weather was too hot. Traveling even for the sake of business was too much work for him!

Meanwhile, my son had joined the school in India. Difference in culture and environment made him feel uneasy in beginning but with my motivation, he somehow adapted. Seven months had passed and I again insisted that my husband should check on the progress of things. Since, we had invested a huge amount of money; we are required to know every intricacy of work. That is when my husband realized that none of the things were working and it was not a profitable deal. He reached back home to tell us the news and decides to go back to Canada.

> *To my shock and surprise, I stood up*
> *(for the first time in life) and said 'NO'.*
>
> *This was my Mona-Vated Moment!*

The same man who spoke so highly of India, just a few months back was saying bad things about the people of this country. It is surprising how Perceptions change and in return change the very course of our Lives.

The Power of Changing Perception is very strong. You cannot fight with it, you cannot go against it. Finally, your perception is your reality. Any traumatic experience can have such an enduring and profound effect on a person's life that even after years; he/she will perceive the environment/place in the similar manner. However, as much as I knew about changing perceptions, I also knew about making small but significant changes to my thoughts to change the reality!

> *It is not the country who makes us what we are. Instead it is what*
> *we bring to the country that makes us who we are!*

I did not have any complaints against India or people residing here. In fact, I was proud of the fact that my son could finally see the real essence of Indian culture. The business did not work because of certain shortcomings but it was a sheer mistake as we did not evaluate the whole picture correctly. Obviously, these thoughts did not resonate with my husband and he had made a firm belief that we can never do well in India. Likewise, he had made the decision to go back.

This time, I was sure what I wanted. I asked him to go back while I would stay in India till my son finishes his ongoing semester. During a brief conversation with my son, he had expressed his desire to finish his present grade. He did not want to give up in the middle of the year. At that moment, my husband packed his bags leaving me and my son behind as he thought he was not meant to be in this country!

Chapter 12
When The Soul Whispers….
Just Listen!

You were born with wings; why prefer to crawl through life?

Rumi

For the first time, I felt free. I felt so light and easy in life. I could spend quality time with myself. The search for a soul purpose drifted me into a different direction.

Even though I was born in India, I had left at such a young age. As a result, I was not in touch with any of my relatives in India. Since, most of my relatives and friends were in Punjab while I was living in Delhi, I was all alone in this city. All I knew was my son and my dog.

One thing that kept me unshaken was – questioning the purpose of my life

As I had begun to question the meaning of my life; everything else became secondary!

I kept asking the vital questions of life—What happened? How did I end up here?

Life was changing in its own subtle ways. I had always expected the unexpected. Changing circumstances had always brought me some new Discoveries about Life. Few days later, I got a call from our landlord saying that our cheque had bounced. That's when I came to know that my husband had taken all the money with him and left nothing for me and my son in India. I went to the bathroom at 3 am in morning and cried like a baby!

I felt helpless and shattered. I had the running expenses of my home and responsibility of my boy and his ongoing studies. In a city which was unknown and unexplored, I did not know where to go and how to re-start my life! My continuous questioning and introspection definitely revealed to me the 'Design of Life' but I was still not able to locate the missing gaps in this jigsaw puzzle.

Just when I kept asking –

"Why me?"

"Why did I have to undergo all this?"

A voice whispered in my ear.

Little inner voice that said "MEDITATE"

The message was clear. It was so audible and profound that I can still feel the word ringing like a bell in my ears. I immediately stopped crying, got up and went back to my bed!

A new Beginning awaited me. I did not know anything about Meditation. I was not even familiar with any of the processes. All I knew was 'Being Open'. I was willing to do anything to help myself come out of the situation. Though I have always been high on energy, sitting quietly to listen to my inner voice marked the start of new chapter in my life.

My husband reached Canada while I had started my Journey!

Since his perspective changed spontaneously, he had no regard left for this country or its people. He felt there were only corrupt and dishonest people in India. Every day, he called to say that we must come back. However, Life had planned something different for us in India.

Next morning, I had to get up at 5 am to meditate. As a young child, I had always heard that this is the best time to meditate as Cosmic Energy is high during Sunrise. But since I was not accustomed to this routine, I kept sleeping. I felt exasperated with myself as I had to somehow take the first step towards growth. I had to find my Mona-Vated Moment because I was sure that Meditation had answers hidden for me. The same day, I went to see a yoga instructor. His centre was very close from where we lived!

I had a crystal clear conversation with him! Firstly, I would require a personal training. Secondly, I would to schedule the class at 4 am in morning. I shall be visiting his centre every morning for classes. Third and most importantly, I will be able to pay him the fees after one month. To my surprise, he agreed to all the terms. I spoke with so much conviction and determination as if there was nothing stopping me!

I had to bring some discipline into my Life. And I felt Yoga will be the right thing at the present moment. I specifically mentioned about coming to his centre for learning as this will make me more committed towards the act. Yoga class from 4 am to 5 am followed by meditation from 5 am onwards. This will be the perfect way to start my day!

Next day, I had the yoga session from 4 am to 4:45 am followed by Meditation (not knowing what to do and how to do?). I just sat and tried bring my focus on breathe. *'Will this calm my mind?'* I asked to myself. But the thoughts of son's fees, money for household expenses, future apprehensions, all clouded my mind very fearlessly. **How will I meditate with so many worries and apprehensions around?**

I was trying to calm a turbulent mind. But I was sure that I will not give up!

Yoga and Meditation kept going on. It had now become a part of my schedule. Days passed but nothing was shifting. I did not feel any substantial change. However, the next day itself my mother showed up in my meditation. It was a vivid visualization. She had a very peaceful and serene conversation with me –

Do you remember how I brought fresh flowers at home when you were a child?

I replied 'Yes'

I want you to bring flowers into your Life.

I was so overwhelmed with her presence and the beautiful message that she gave. Immediately, I got up and walked out of my home looking for a street florist. I found one who had a small shop few blocks down the street. Since, he was the nearest florist, I asked him to deliver fresh flowers to my home, twice a day. It made me laugh inside when I told him that I will pay him towards the end of the month. No money, no source of income but I had started my journey with some assurance from God that it will be done anyhow.

To my astonishment, he also agreed to the deal.

Happy Moments, praise God

Difficult Moments, seek God

Quiet Moments, worship God

Painful Moments, trust God

Every Moment, thank God

A Street vendor for whom every penny matters agreed to take the money later. This was a re-assurance that I am going in the right direction!

The florist came the same day and put beautiful lilies and roses in my home!

Suddenly, the place became energized. It gave calmness to the atmosphere. I could feel the cloud of apprehension and worry being cleared slowly. Meditation continued in its own beautiful manner. In fact, it was now my visions were taking their own beautiful course.

Chapter 13
Find Peace and Freedom in Heart

As the Meditation continued, my connection with my mom and universal voice grew deeper. The next message that I received was to spend more and more time with Nature.

Being around the trees, feeling the roots was required since so long. So, yet again, without wasting a single minute, I got ready after finishing the meditation and boarded the bus which took me to near-by garden. I would spend 4-5 hours over there till my son returned from school. In every walk in Nature, I could release most of my traumatic or unpleasant memories of the past. While surrounding myself with Earth Energies, I could feel the warmth and calmness entering inside my system!

It seemed as if Nature was stabilizing me.

Connect with Nature and it will keep your Trust that all is well.

Slowly, all the judgments that occupied my mind were fading away. I was feeling lighter and lighter as I visited that Garden each morning. I could release the energy of forgiveness against all those who had caused me pain. This indeed was the biggest gift of Nature. I felt as if I had released myself from a cage that I had purposely built for myself.

With each inhale, I could lift my heart closer to the Universe!

Even people working in the Botanical Garden became friends with me. We exchanged smiles as I entered the Garden, took strolls around, hugged trees and sat close to the roots. However, they were decent enough not to disturb me while I carried all these rituals with Nature. There was a day in between when I feel sick. That morning, I could not visit the Garden. I was feeling very weak so I decided to stay at home and give rest to my body. However, as the evening arrived, I started feeling uneasy. I kept walking around the home as I missed walking in the Garden. It was 7 pm already but I started to feel as if somebody was waiting for me. I missed being around the trees so much that I finally took a bus even though it was late evening. I finally reached my sacred place and spent around 30 minutes with Nature before ending the day!

Love for Nature and Meditation also brought in a special gift in Life. Little did I know that I would cherish this gift till the end of my Life.

In one of the Meditation session, I saw the presence of my Guardian Angels.

They appeared in a tranquil state. They humbly said --- whatever you need; we will provide you!

The presence of Energy was so overwhelming that I knew there was someone who protected me watched over me and my family. Even when I would have bills in my hand while sitting on the table, I use to put it across the empty chair right in front of me. And I would say out loud to the angels ---

This is your problem. You take care of bills while I work on myself!

BELIEVERS, LOOK UP – TAKE COURAGE. THE ANGELS ARE NEARER THAN YOU THINK.

Billy Graham

While I was noticing a big shift in my Life, I saw across a title while visualizing. It was called *'One Soul Many Lives'*. Next thing I knew was looking for such a title in book stores across Connaught Place. One of the famous book stores at that time was 'Om Book Store'. As I entered inside, I felt confused and perplexed.

Do I ask for such a title?

Does such a book even exist or was it my imagination?

Will it sound funny if I ask the shop manager?

I was apprehensive but asked the shopkeeper somehow. He nodded his head saying that the book is not available at the present moment but they might receive the stock soon!

I was astonished and dumbstruck --- **From where is all this information being loaded in my mind?**

However, I got out of the book store feeling thrilled that I shall be able to read the book soon. A part of me was also feeling sad as I could not find the book today itself. I had to take a right turn to reach home but not knowing why, I took a left instead. After driving a few blocks, I stopped at one of the red lights. While I am floating in my own thoughts waiting for the signal to get green, I hear a sudden knock on my window. A road side vendor stood there holding a bunch of books and magazines in his hand.

Wow... the first book amongst them was 'One Soul Many Lives' by Roy Stemman

It was unbelievable. I was literally dancing while sitting on the driver's seat.

There was a sheer enthusiasm and happiness as I immediately bought the book from him!

When the Student is Ready; the Teacher will Appear ~~ Buddhist Proverb

I knew the book was not genuine but I was not just carrying the book but also taking home –

My Trust in Angels

Chapter 14
Wake Up! Life gives you Multiple Chances…
Life will pay you exactly what you ASK for!

My immediate concern was 'generation of funds'. I had to get a regular source of income anyhow. The running expenses needed to be taken care of so I asked. I asked my angels that 'I need to generate money' but I don't know how to compete with the growing economy and society. Any decent job in Delhi, at that time required a minimum MBA qualification.

Since my education was not up to the standards, it was less likely to get a well-paying job.

I might not have had anything in my hand but with Meditation I surely had the clarity over two things—One, I wanted to do something that only brings positive people in my life and secondly, my work should help me get closer to my purpose of soul searching.

I always liked to Motivate others as I did for myself! Towards the end, we all share the same journey and I feel sharing my own experiences with Life will help others find their own Path.

All my discoveries and new insights were coming through in that hour which I dedicated to Meditation. As I kept the intention for job/work/money, I was asked to go online and look for relevant organizations in and around Delhi. I was Guided to look more deeper into 'Law of Attraction' and find relevant courses or groups!

I was a firm believer of the 'Law of Attraction'. My guardian angels also reminded me of the same. As I searched online, I found a person who was hosting workshops around Spirituality and also handled Law of Attraction groups.

After 2 days, we met over coffee and I shared my life story with him. I told him that I always attracted what I wanted and I could understand the working of 'Law of Attraction' at a deeper level. After hearing all of it, he had a subtle smile on his face. He giggled and said, 'The Universe was waiting for you'. He had started a 'Law of Attraction' group long time back but there was no appropriate facilitator/trainer to lead that group.

Following the thoughts and conversation, he immediately proposed that I should design a workshop around 'Law of Attraction' in India. And he decided that we should keep it as 3 Day Training Program. Even before I blinked my eyes, he started spreading the word and registering people for the same. People started to pay in advance to book their seats while I had no idea of what I would do in those 3 crucial days!

Through the support of Meditation, I designed a 3 days interactive workshop for participants.

The core purpose was to share my learnings with others; to empower those who felt stuck at a particular point in life. 'Law of Attraction' is always an individual journey. Each one of us comes to earth with a desire in our Heart. And passion to follow that with desire is already inbuilt within us! All we need to do is keep moving ahead without losing focus and attention. Our sole purpose is to --

'Live to our full potential'

Therefore, with these three days, my task was to remind all my participants about their dreams. A lot of the exercises were also designed around the challenges that Life keeps throwing at us. But we must grow out of those and keep moving ahead without any excuses.

My Life was defined by struggles and great number of risks that I took just to see a new perspective. So during the workshop, I asked my participants to do the same.

Exploring, Discovering and Challenging Life!

While I am traveling on my path authentically, I will automatically Discover what is Effective and what is ineffective in my Life. But all of this can only be possible through Inner Motivation.

By God's Grace, each of the participants was responsive to the workshop and exercises conducted during the three days. Most of them experienced a Great Shift in their thought process. So by the end of third day, all 30 participants were ready to pay more fees and wanted to continue for another 3 days!

Let me share with you another profound insight. While we had started marketing for the workshop, I was required to give some inputs that stated my credibility. I was absolutely new to this field with no previous experience of training programs. Therefore, there were no testimonials that would instill faith in people for me and my work. The only person who believed in my work was my Son. My nine year old son had seen my journey and had experienced tremendous growth and learning while he walked along with me.

I feel proud to say that in times of major upheaval and unrest, most of the inner work happens. With my guidance, he went through an inner development that was far beyond the capability of a 9 year old.

He sat in front of the camera and spoke out his heart!
He was my first and most powerful testimonial.

Chapter 15
Law of Perception
There is No Need to Rush. If something is meant to be, it will happen.

In the right time, with the right person, for the Best Reason!

I connected with the person who infused the energy of *'becoming a Trainer'* within me. I was introduced to a huge array of Social Media. It changed my Life drastically. I was now able to connect to a large number of people. Personal Growth and great Accomplishments followed after I got exposed to facebook and other online marketing tools. My personality was enhanced and I felt more confident while delivering any of the talks.

Just before my first workshop, I stayed up all night to meditate and bring all my energies in alignment with Process of 'Law of Attraction'. I made sure that the total number of participants should not exceed 30. I was keen and willing to give personal attention to each and every one of the participants. I felt a deep compassion as I knew I had traveled the same path.

Just as every snowflake is unique, every person is unique!

And I wanted each one of them to be Open and explore the endless possibilities that world offers them. The workshop was a great success. The news about 'Law of Attraction' spread like wildfire; some of them even traveled from far distant corners of India just to be a part of this training.

Just when the workshop was gaining momentum, I was approached by Times of India. One of their reporters wanted to interview me and publish the article in next edition. I was thrilled and felt honored. My voice was reaching out to more and more people. And helping them overcome big or even small stumbling blocks in life. Just as we started with the interview, I received a call from Sandeep Ji saying there is a problem but it's a good problem!

We had organized an introductory program in an auditorium. The hall could occupy 30-40 people but we received mind boggling news that the total count of people had gone to 150. So we had to change the venue and instead look for a bigger seminar hall.

It was a Great Eye Opener for me. India was moving towards Self-Growth and Self-Enhancement. People were becoming more and more open to training programs, therapies, processes and workshop formats.

On the day of seminar, I saw my interview published in newspaper. The process of Law of Attraction was extensively mentioned there. I was feeling great energy and enthusiasm as Life was offering me beautiful opportunities! Just as I began the seminar, a memory came flashing before my eyes—

My Mona-Vated Moment.

Few years back, as I did my routine job in Canada, I visualized that someday, I would visit India and facilitate the people here.

Since I always felt close to my roots, there was deep desire to work for a great cause and upliftment of society!

Coming back to the personal life, my husband knew that the workshops were being really appreciated and promoted around the city. On one of the days, when we were registering people for the next program, I received a call from him. Instead of appreciating my efforts, he commented that participants were more interested in my looks rather than self-growth process!

At that moment, I was surprised and furious at his remarks but today as I look back, I forgive him for all his sayings. An individual's behavior is primarily determined by his perception of the world. He is simply a by-product of his beliefs. Once it is formed, it influences every area of his life. For example, before coming to India, my husband had a very good and clean perception about the country and its people. Suddenly, when the perception changed, he took a flight back, leaving everything behind unfinished.

Perceptions change from time to time. Sometimes we do not have any control over them. They act as external stimuli. They can invoke various emotions within us. So I learnt that the best technique is to focus your attention on your experiences and building your own reality!

While meditating, I always had a perception that I am going to attract only those who are really willing to transform lives.

YOU ATTRACT WHAT YOU ARE

NOT WHAT YOU WANT

IF YOU WANT TO ATTRACT GREAT;

THEN BE GREAT.

Chapter 16
Giving Birth to a 'Visionary Genius'

All the workshop participants were extremely happy with the changes that followed after being a part of the training program. Few of them requested me to start programs with children or specifically teenagers. I had seen my son grow old amidst so many issues and family turbulences. Yet my intervention always helped him look at the broader perspectives of Life. I could feel the sensitivity of a child and I was very thrilled to introduce a program where the teenagers or even toddlers would benefit from Law of Attraction Process.

That's when I gave birth to a class called 'Visionary Genius'. Here I invited the children of all the participants who had attended my programs. 15 kids attended the first class of 'Visionary Genius'. They were from an age group of 5 to 18 years. My aim was to empower them with skills that they will cherish for life. There were multiple facets to the training but some of the key elements were – *Expressing effectively with Parents, Teachers, peer groups; channelizing their energies; and finally changing thoughts into reality.*

All the training was imparted through fun games and various exercises. Children have a lot of energy and it needs to be dissipated in the right manner that also ensures some learning. So I was sure that the only way to teach children was introducing—Mindful Exercises

Initially, they were closed. A training program is not a child's first choice. Instead he would always choose a more leisure activity.

However, by afternoon, all the kids were extremely motivated and excited to be doing more and more activities. By the evening, they hugged me, kissed me, some of them even cried. The older kids expressed that this training was better than the Graduation Moment for them.

For me, it was the most overwhelming moment of my Life.

My Mona-Vated Moment.

You can be in the Darkest phase of your Life but the moment you see child-like innocence, it changes your whole perception of your Life. Immediately, you see a light amongst the dark clouds. You even be the light for others!

As I saw their radiant faces, I was sure that these children were on the path of Happiness and also practicing Healthy Lifestyle Choices.

Chapter 17
Inner Journey with my Son

This chapter specifically narrates the Journey with my Son.

> *Children can change your Life ---*
> *Absolutely, Definitely, Positively*

Since childhood, I had always asked for my purpose. I felt special for many reasons. However, the circumstances around did not allow me to explore my full potential and work towards a goal in Life. I attained maturity at a very early age. My mother's demise, moving away from my native land, an early job, all of this strengthened me but I also missed the essence of being innocent and acting foolish as a child.

Like any other parent, I wanted to give the best to my child and specifically, letting him enjoy his childhood immensely.

> *The only way to bless your Child is –*
> *Offer him a Happy Childhood*

At our times, we were given specific directions in Life. And we were just supposed to follow in robot-like ways. However, times keep changing. Children today are impulsive and yet creative. They intend to learn through their own life. As parents, one should make sure that we start their education as early as possible. But this is not the formal education; instead it is the practical education where the child discovers the dynamics of his personality, emotions, and his relationships in day to day life.

Childhood is the Golden Period of our Life. It should be a period of freedom, enjoyment with an absence of responsibilities. As "Experience is the Best Teacher", we just need to provide a conducive and safe environment to child where he discovers more of himself. As a mother, I had desired to give the same environment to my child.

When I saw that my job consumed too much of time and energy, I decided to quit and instead find work that allows me to spend enough and more beautiful time with my son.

From the early days, Paras (my son) had the ability to view the world from a very different lens. When he was 5 year old, he created a project at school called – 'To Think Is to Create'. Under this project, he created Colorful Pencil Holders (using foam cups), decorated them with glitters and wrote life virtues on them. Then he decided to display these products at various fairs and festivals at a very marginal price. He was even awarded 'The Top Entrepreneur' for creating such a concept.

Yet another achievement was raising funds for his school. He took part in a contest where children were supposed to raise maximum funds (to buy a pet). He reached home with basket of tickets that needed to be sold. At age 7, he volunteered to call all my friends on his own and begin a conversation where he explained them about the cause and ensure that the basket is sold. Just after 2 calls, he was able to sell 2 baskets.

As I heard one of his conversations, I was amazed at his skill. He began by saying ---

'How many baskets would you like?'

'By the way, one is not an option'.

For me, this was 'thinking out of the box'. In no time, he sold 20 baskets and collected maximum amount of money for the charity. As a token of appreciation, he was gifted a Nike Bag that he stills keeps as ***the most cherished memory***.

Paras had attended all my workshops and training programs. He is always focused towards doing things differently. One of his other enthusiastic projects was when he decided to sell his old DVD's and CD's. For the same, he designed a ¾ size board, carried it to the street and stood there waiting for passer-by to stop and buy his merchandise.

Young Minds working is definitely Rewarding. It helps the Child tap into his/her problem-solving skills and develop a strong Emotional Wellbeing!

Every time, he earned money from any of these projects, he donated a part of it to support the homeless. While we stayed in India, he became my biggest support and motivation. There were times when I felt very lonely and alienated in the country with no money and a big responsibility to raise my kid. But as I experienced the dip, he would jump in front of me and say ---

"Mom, if you can do it once. You can do it many times".

When I had my first encounter with angels, he felt uneasy about the whole incident. But later he realized the presence of energies. He knew that we were protected by higher energies and they always come to us when we need them the most!

Each child is unique; he brings with him a very distinctive yet special set of skills. So there is no 'ideal' environment that ensures well-being and healthy growth for child. But yes, we all must ensure that we understand childhood, focus on the specific needs of the child and then allow him to play and explore the world with growing wisdom.

If you are a parent; open doors to unknown directions to the child so that he can explore. Don't make him afraid of the unknown, give him support

OSHO

When a child explores on his own, he starts to question but he also generates an answer immediately. And that answer is born out of his child-like innocence.

I was stepping into a very crucial state of my Life. I had decided to end the relationship with my husband. The process of Divorce had already begun. Since I had undergone trauma and pain, I would cry separately, secretly, trying to hide my feelings from my son. But he would always hear me sobbing and ensure that I feel better and say *'we would do better now'*. He felt the pain and even questioned the whole dynamics of his relationship with his father. Deep inside, he started to believe that his father was not fair towards him. But each night before sleeping, we would sit together and pray for his well-being.

One of the nights, Paras asked, *'Why do we pray for his well-being when we he did bad things to us'*. That is when I imparted him with the lesson on Forgiveness. Forgiveness simply means you accept the person as he is. At that moment, there was a Deep Sense of Connection between me and my child. Words cannot describe it. But I knew that my son had found the peace within!

One of the other days, he asked me a very vital question.

What is the way out of Labyrinth?

'Labyrinth'....???'

Well, I had never heard the word before. So first, I checked for the meaning online.

'Labyrinth' is another word for a Maze (technically defined as a network of paths and hedges designed as a puzzle through which one has to find a way).

On further questioning, he said,

'*How do we let go of things that just need to go from our life?*'

When a child questions the deeper aspects of Life, just remember, he is moving towards Freedom and external Happiness.

I was stupefied with the wisdom of a 12 year old who wanted to free himself of all the drama around. And was willing to start afresh!

One of the most important questions that I always asked Paras was – **What are you here for?**

Please look into it deeply.

I asked him 'What are you here for?' rather than asking 'What do you want to be?'

In my opinion, this question will let the child explore **'what is possible'** than **'what is tagged, labeled and available'**.

Don't encourage them to copy someone. ***Don't Raise a Robot; Raise a Visionary.***

Chapter 18
Do Not Discount What a Child Says!

Life is a series of natural and spontaneous changes. Resisting those changes is foolish. Since we all go through the ***ebb and flow***; the best way is to embrace both the realities and keep flowing ahead!

Whenever I had to fight through some bad days, I asked God for Strength, Courage and that keeps me Alive and moving ahead.

~ Life Begins where Fear Ends ~

OSHO

But it is easy to discount fear when everything is functioning normally. The real challenge takes place when you have no other choice other than accepting all your fears and overcoming them with Courage. On one of the days, when life was being hard on me and my emotions were pulling me into a dark valley, I prayed to God and asked for Courage!

I had to overcome the situation. I wanted to!

The only way out was to ask for 'Courage' and sleep; hoping that next day will offer a new light and new strength to face the ebb and flow of life!

I woke up the next morning. As I was preparing breakfast, my son came down and randomly asked me --- *"Mom, do you know how God gives you Courage?"*

I was perplexed. ASKING FOR….. COURAGE….. GOD….. This was too much of a coincidence!

I thought to myself ---

How could my son come up with the same thought the next day morning?

Even before, I could answer to my son's question. He said,

'GOD doesn't give you the Courage. He gives you the circumstances so that you become courageous'.

My Mona-Vated Moment came rushing towards me!

But this time it was my Son who came as a Messenger. He gave me the biggest gift – a *perspective*.

Life offers opportunities to strengthen you; to make you more Courageous. But sadly, we misinterpret and seek for the strengths secretly at night. While the real power and valor is already available to us abundantly. We are just supposed to use it at right time in Life!

My Child passed on the most beautiful message to me. Children in their sheer innocence offer a lot of necessary knowledge free from any conditioning. It is on us whether we pay attention to it or just discard it casually!

Chapter 19
Closure on the Relationship
Closure!

We all seek it. We seek the end of things and also the beginning of new things. Those things we can't find closure on haunt us. They pop up in our dreams, and creep into our thoughts in idle moments, like a mind-bender.

I was very comfortable with Life. My work and my inner journey were together taking me to another dimension. All along, the bond with my son deepened. It all looked fair and fancy now. But I was mistaken. How far can I go forward when the past strings are still holding me tightly?

My husband went back to Canada leaving the family behind. This gave me a chance to move ahead and seek happiness and peace within myself. But I did not want to leave my relationship as an 'Unfinished Business'. I owed an apology to myself as I was unfair to my life and well-being. I was always concerned about the 'other' in relationship. But the transformational days spent in India made me realize my worth.

Anger, Resentment, Betrayal, Anxiety, all of these heavy emotions were oozing out while I meditated during my stay in India. I was sure that NOW I had to work on myself. I did not need any answers or explanations from my partner. Regardless of what he has done, I am going to free myself from those thoughts/memories.

I started doing a practice --- that worked as a great therapeutic tool for me.

I started writing letters to my husband. Each day, I wrote a letter to him expressing all my feelings, anger and sorrows. It worked as deep catharsis. In the end, I would just fold the letter and keep it inside. I never posted any of these letters but they all helped me in releasing a lot of emotions on paper. With the release of emotions, I felt calmer and peaceful with my husband.

What I saw as the biggest betrayal in my life NOW appeared as the biggest Blessing.

People keep coming and going in our lives but we must attach ourselves to only the Experience instead of the individual.

In fact, those who hurt us or bring pain to us are truly the Masters from our previous lives.

After 2 years of staying in India, I moved back to Canada. At that time, I did not know that I was being prepared for another big shock. I came back to the house that we owned in the past. That was the only house we did not sell when we moved to India. So I moved back and stayed in one small room while my husband and his parents occupied all the other rooms and used the huge house to their maximum comfort.

As I am settling myself back in Canada, I received stacks and stacks of letters from the creditors. They all were bills. Bills of purchases that I was completely unaware of! I had paid off everything before I left for India.

I could feel that there was big trouble coming my way. I was the primary card holder and account holder since I had come to Canada first while my husband was the second holder to the account. I added his name after we got married. So obviously, I was reliable for everything. We were also doing a lot of real estate deals together before leaving for India. Every deal, I signed the papers trusting him and his ability to crack the deal. Only later did I come to know that some of those deals had gone wrong. Due to which creditors from government were sending in letters.

I have been living in Canada for so long and I had maintained a very good credit history. I was never declined for any loan because of my long lasting credit line up. However, now I owed so much money to the bank and creditors that I did not know what to do!

I desperately required an explanation for all the expenses and unpaid bills that were made on my name. On questioning my husband, he said, '*Looking at the condition and huge amounts of debts, you will have to file up for bankruptcy. Some more expenses and purchases will not make any difference*'.

He was spending money ruthlessly thinking that it will all be taken care off when I declare bankruptcy. At that point, I felt so helpless. I did not have any savings from my work in India. Whatever I earned was only enough to take care of running expenses. As I reached Canada, I was only left with 20$ in my pocket.

It's not going to be Easy; it's going to be really hard.
We will have to work at this together!

All I wanted to hear were these simple lines. This simple sentence shows how you can overcome any trouble just because you are accompanied by your loved ones.

For the first time, I approached my Dad. I wanted to seek his help and guidance. On my own, I felt so lost once AGAIN. What I thought I had overcome was actually coming back to me…. this time wearing a different mask!

Even in the deepest agony, my Mona-Vated Moment
somehow arrived ---

Life is not something that you Master at one point and you think that chapter is over. Instead it is continuous journey.

I realized that there is another Blessing coming up in here. But I did not know what was it?

So I tried Stay Positive and Calm but YES, Honestly, I also felt Disoriented and Lost Again!

How could be I in this relationship when so much of damage had already been done?

Till how long can we wear the façade of love or concern when there was nothing left in heart?

I asked my Dad and he spoke to my husband thinking that together we could fix the situation instead of watching it go bad and then worse.

It was a brief but deep conversation. My father made him realize the importance of his partner. "*She had an amazing job before she married you. She took care of all your needs over many years and supported you in all your endeavors. Now that you are living comfortably in big home with car and all necessities, she needs your support and all the comforts*".

"*Instead she is facing a terrible money crisis and you need to support her now*".

At that point, my husband said, '*I will take care of everything in her life. The only condition is that she should sleep with me*'. I had already mentioned to my dad that I was feeling so weak emotionally, it was impossible to establish a physical relationship at this point of time.

My Dad tried his best to establish peace again. My husband was assured that his wife will come back to him but he needs to take good care of her as she is broken emotionally and mentally. So that needs to be considered as priority.

He agreed to everything that my dad said. As a result my dad was out of the scene and the frame of husband and wife returned. Few days passed, he did not make any initiative of pooling in money or helping me get out of this mess.

My Dad called again to check on the proceedings but I told him there is no change in situation. Thankfully, my son was out of this chaos as he had gone to spend the summer vacations with my sister's kids. I felt very lonely all this while, sitting in the small room with just my suitcase, nobody to talk to, no television, and no radio.

Few days later, he initiated that we should get the car insurance so I went out with him.

He was willing to transfer the old car under my name. The time to pay for Insurance had arrived. He wanted to walk away from it and put the entire burden on me. At this point, calling my dad and asking for money was easy. He could have come to my rescue. He could have paid my car insurance. But I did not want to take any support at this point of time. I instead chose to figure out a solution on my own. I was willing to lose the car or any other belonging. But I would not lose my Integrity at any cost. This bothered him more and he finally said - *'I cannot take care of you. You need to make your own money and take care of your own life'.*

That's the day I realized that this relationship is not worth saving! This is the time when I seriously needed financial and emotional comfort. And he backed off.

Maybe that was his way of controlling the relationship. Maybe he thought that controlling me will enable a smooth relationship but I surely had to make a decision this time!

I called up my Dad and said – I am moving out! I can't take it any longer!

I packed my bags and left for my dad's place. I felt at that moment that this separation is very peaceful. At least there is no drama and chaos about leaving home or him following me, using abusive words.

The Mona-Vated Moment here says ---

At some point, you have to realize that some people can stay in your Heart but not in your Life!

Chapter 20
Stand Up and Re-Start your Life!

YOU CAN'T START THE NEXT CHAPTER OF YOUR LIFE IF YOU KEEP RE-READING THE LAST ONE!

With all my stuff, I moved into a small bachelor room. My dad had a small house in which there was a small bachelor room where I moved in. My dad and step mum were about to go to India for 6 months. So by the time I settled into the house I also started looking for a job in the meantime. Within a month, I got a store manager position with one of the retail companies.

Even though he was my dad, I did not want to become a burden on him so I was paying for my own hydro bill (electricity bill) and small portion of the rent!

Since I had got a job at fast food joint, the store would open as early as 5 am and close down by 1 am. Sometimes, I had to leave home at 4:30 am and I came back by 2:30 am at night.

Paras (my son) had started with his school so he came back from my sister's place. I could not imagine how a 12 year old would cope with parent's separation all by himself; considering that I had long hours at work and he would be all alone at home through the entire day.

God willing, the kid became extremely independent at the age of 12. Even though I went to work at 4 am, he would get up on time, get ready for his school, make breakfast for himself and also walk the dog, and feed the dog before going to school. He would come back from school, again walk the dog, feed him and then eat the lunch that I prepared for him early in the morning. He was sincere in his studies and did not let any of this bother his curriculum. All of it was done in a small room. Both of us lived in a room that was as small as a bathroom or a kitchen. There was no space for me to even put a bed. So we could just fit in one small mattress. From a 6 bedroom, ocean view house to a small room for me and my son!

When life gives you LEMONS; it's time to open the GIN!

I worked very hard for 6 months in order to save a good amount of money. So that I could give up the job and spend more time with my son. I could not see him ignored anymore! In the mean time, my husband had totally pulled the plug from this relationship.

My son didn't want to see his father neither did his father want to see him. A month before my dad came back from India, a major thing happen again. I did not know why I was attracting to get so many shocks. While I was taking shower, the kitchen got on fire. My son immediately noticed it and called me. I came out, we put the fire down but there was too much smoke in the room so I had to call 911. I and my son were rushed to hospital because we had inhaled too much smoke into our body.

We came back home and saw that there was not much damage done but because of smoke the entire walls had turned black. Since, my dad was about to return, I did not want him to see his home in this condition after the mishap took place in my presence. So it would be unfair to let him pay for all the mess. Likewise, I got the whole area painted again; I replaced the cabinets, the appliances. Anything that had got affected even slightly, I replaced all of it.

I knew it was an additional expense but I had no choice.

My dad came back and got the news from my sister. Rather than being worried for us, he was worried that his house had caught fire. He expressed it in a very different way but it almost felt like he was more concerned about the house than his family.

I apologized for the mishap and informed him that I will move out soon! He agreed to the decision.

I did not know where I would go but I had committed to myself that I will move out in next 10-15 days and I did so. Above that, I had also decided to quit my job in the same month as my son needed me more than anyone else. So I moved out and moved into a new place again.

But as promised to myself, I moved into a bigger house and because there was enough space available, I started facilitating group session from my home for meditation and spiritual healing.

Next thing I know, there were 10-15 people who came in for the first class at 5 am.

All you Need to Do --- SEND MESSAGE TO THE UNIVERSE.

Every day, at 5 am I had 10-15 people who came for meditation. Eventually I was running 3 groups in a day, one at 5 am, next 6 am and last one at 7 am.

Going back to my relationship, my husband had initiated a meeting with me. He wanted to initiate peace for the well-being of our son. So I went to meet him. Even at this time, I was thinking that maybe there will be universal light showered on this relationship.

While we are sitting in the restaurant and having food, he commented, *'What have you decided?*

Are you coming back?'

Before I could say anything he said, *'I cannot feed Paras all by myself (the father and son were meeting each other every second weekend, as per court orders). I need someone to cook and clean and do the daily chores'.*

I don't want a man who loves me because he needs me.

Instead I wanted to be with someone who needs me because he loves me.

Maybe I should release him and also give him a chance to find someone who will suit his needs and personality. I could not offer that relationship anything now! I had lost a lot anyways!

I finally told him, 'Let's part our ways'. You can get married again and live a more peaceful life.

Within a month, he sent me the divorce papers.

Within that year, we were divorced. As per the child care support, he gave me only 200$ as child support. I chose to walk away from the big house that we owned together. Everything that we owned together, I walked away from it all and I let him have it.

Sometimes you must let go and dare to do it because life is too short to wonder about what could have happened if I had withheld on those things.

Peace was way more important than verbal abuse or any other materialistic drama. I was willing to let go of anything that would bring me down emotionally. Not even once did I feel anger, resentment or blame towards my ex-husband because I was tuned into the Universal Vibration now. I knew all this had happened for a reason. I was able to let go in a beautiful way.

One of the days my son asked, '*how can you forgive him so easily? He has not been good to us. Why do we send him silent love each night?*'

If we hold on to grudge, anger or bad feelings, we will be chained into our own thoughts and will never move ahead. So the best thing is to replace the feeling of hatred with the feelings of love.

The more you send love, the more you will free yourself from every emotion. Years down the lane, when we look back, you will realize how precious this experience was!

This is definitely a Blessing!

My son definitely learnt the **Art of Forgiveness** and the **Art of Having Healthy Relationships**; with his dad and others around. No matter what he does, he will still remain your dad.

The Closure came finally!

Paras asked for the answers and he got it.

His Mona-Vated Moment---

Only when you seek the truth, it is gradually revealed!

My 12 year old son was open to the new learning and most of all; he was willing to free himself.

Are you willing to free yourself of all the shackles of the past?

Are you willing to surround yourself only with people who are going to take you higher?

Chapter 21
Love For Sisters

"We hang out, we help one another, we tell one another our worst fears and biggest secrets, and then just like real sisters, we listen and don't judge."

Adriana Trigiani

Sisters may be the women who grew up under the same roof or they may be dear friends that you met along the way. I was blessed with both.

Having two elder sisters means immense protection, care, nurturing throughout my childhood. Siblings can share childhood memories with you that no one else can connect to in quiet a similar way. Your sister may drive you crazy or she may inspire you but finally you share the feeling of womanhood together. Every girl goes through a transformation and steps into the womanhood with certain difficulties and emotional cauldron. This is the time when sisters may inspire you; assist you or at least listen to your ease and pain.

Maybe you have an older sibling you look to for guidance, or maybe you have a younger sister who is looking to you for inspiration. But finally, I would say that Sisterhood is a very special relationship and you must celebrate it all through your life.

My Journey might help you find perspective on your relationship when you are feeling troubled. But I would only request you to be Transparent about what you feel. Find Words and Make Time to express your Feelings to your Sisters. This will not only Strengthen your Bond but also help you establish better relationships with other women in Life… as you grow older!

As I mentioned before, we were three sisters born and brought up against all odds of society. We were raised beautifully by our mother. She always believed that if she has given birth to three daughters, there has to be a Divine reason behind it. While she struggled with her illness, all three sisters distributed the household tasks amongst each other. When our mother grew extremely weak, she could not stand up and go the washroom on her own. That is when all of us nursed her while she lay on bed.

Every relationship that I mention about has Authenticity and Integrity. This authenticity does not come from others but your own self being. How transparent you are decides the intensity of your relationship with another! If I am fair and straightforward in my conduct, and speak the truth in all varieties of communication – verbal or nonverbal; I will lay the foundation of the strongest relationship that I will cherish for life. This is a one point formula for any relationship to flourish in its full glory.

It can be your partners, lovers, parents, siblings, soul friends or children. It may be the longest relationships of your life or shortest. But remember to stay 'Honest'. And 'honest' here specifically means 'communicating your truth' and your 'genuine feelings' to the other. This ensures a constant flow of energy and love amongst each other.

The Sibling Bond may be called as the 'longest relationship' of your life. It is the one that gives you as much grief as pleasure. Though there is not much research done on it but my insights on a sibling bond only flow out of my own life experiences. This is in fact the only relationship that involves shared upbringing, shared genes and shared secrets. As you grow older, you realize the importance of having a friendly sibling for companionship, reminiscences (as the stories of family holidays are boring for someone else) and practical support.

In this seesaw of sibling relationship, it gets more intense when there are only sisters. Amongst the sisters, it is both closest and competitive. The psychologist Robert Williams described it as varying through life: 'In childhood, a girl may view her older sister as rival; when puberty approaches, the sister becomes an admirable guide to the adolescent world; shortly thereafter, when both are receiving boy's attention, the sister may again become an unwelcome competitor.'

This is a really interesting study but what really fills my heart is the love that sisters share as they get older. The support that comes from your parents suddenly starts flowing from your sisters. They may be elder or younger to you but suddenly the powerful emotional center shifts to your sisters. They assist you over various matters, act like a strong sounding board, remind you of your family wisdom and laugh over childhood memories. All these help us connect back to our family roots. Psychologically, we feel extremely secure and comforted by supporting siblings.

As I was going through a tough phase of separation with my ex-husband, I was relieved and assured because my son was comforted by my sister accompanied by her children during summer holidays. The family structure and bonding was extremely critical for my 9 year old son. I feel blessed to have a family who supported me and my son at the time of crisis. I'd like to focus on only the positive aspects so I will not talk about the petty fights that sisters have while they are growing up. Instead, I would only talk about the importance of womanhood and 'Art of relating to women' that comes when you have a healthy relationship with your sisters.

As a girl, when we talk to our sisters, we get a wider perspective of life and emotions. On the contrary, an unhealthy relationship with sisters leads to co-dependence on friends, female colleagues and female teachers. A love-hate relationship which is pre-dominant in sisters is searched for outside. Women start to model or mirror other females in an unhealthy manner. One seeks for self-approval outside extensively.

Healthy Relationship creates Happiness and Well-Being. And the Sisters specifically act as Magical Mirrors. We can see who we truly are. She sees the Best in Us and also brings out the Strongest Emotion. A study in the Journal Child Development analyzed interviews with the parents and first and second born children in 200 families. It was found that sisters feel closer to their siblings than brother do.

Other studies have also revealed that the sister herself served as a replacement for the primary relationship. Sisters are well- aware of each other's physical health and illness. This awareness itself serves as a catalyst for greater contact. A woman who responds to her family and siblings in early childhood is later able to assume increased responsibility and protectiveness with her partner and new family. Women's desire for Healing and Compassion is deeply rooted in their very being. But early bonding with family and particularly sisters in her family builds enhanced sense of sensitivity within her!

Healthy relationship with sisters will lead to healthy state of womanhood.

My Mona-Vated Moment here is very unique and overwhelming. But I am going to share it a little later. Just in some time. Before that, I will share another element of my life with you. My dad got married the second time. That's when we welcomed the fourth sister in our family. Since I was the youngest, I always enjoyed the love and attention and pampering given to the youngest lass of the family. I always felt special that way. However, when we had the newest member arrive home, as much as I was thrilled and excited, I also felt threatened. Somewhere, I wasn't able to accept that the title of youngest will now be given to the other kid. I will not call it as being mature or immature. It is simply a play of emotions. We all feel loved, appreciated, deprived, threatened, fearful, and angry, or overwhelmed. These are just emotional structures within us.

Feelings are much like waves, we can't stop them from coming but we can choose which one to surf.

When things don't go the way we want them to; we find it hard to accept! We become adamant and stubborn. Somewhere we forget that the very essence of life is 'newness'. At every point of time, something new is added to your life. A new experience, a new person, a new emotion, a new outlook to life; every step that we take is new. Scientifically speaking, our cells regenerate on their own and take a new form each day. We just feel a little insecure while stepping into the new. That is the only fear or apprehension. Shift your outlook and see every new experience as an opportunity. I went through a massive transformation after this episode.

It completely changed my perception. I started seeing life by stepping into other's shoes. I questioned my own feelings, my fears and soon realized that each one carries a story. Maybe our fourth sister who now becomes the youngest lass carries her own memories. She has different view towards life and being part of this family. I started feeling more love and acceptance towards all in the family. The sheer empathy and compassion for others made me transparent towards life and emotions.

~ The appearance of things changes according to the emotions; and thus we see magic and beauty in them, while the magic and beauty are really in ourselves. ~

Khalil Gibran

Each one lives with their pain, sorrows, happiness, sadness and while living a life with a myriad of emotions, we put on various masks. Most of the times, people are not willing to remove these masks. They meet you, chill out with you, share their worries or happy moments, but deep inside, they still put on these masks. You cannot see the authenticity of others unless they are really open to you. So as a therapist and a compassionate woman, I learned the art of looking at what lies beneath their masks.

I accepted them as they are!

This acceptance is the only true wisdom. If we accept the person, situation, ourselves, anything that is around, the way it is, without manipulating or changing, and then we start to move towards leading a real Authentic and Spiritual Life!

Accept the fact that you can't control everything, and not everything can go the way you want it to. Choose instead, to find the positive in every situation.

Everyone carries the world within themselves. Each one wants the things to work exactly the way, they have thought in their mind. This is the real cause of suffering. The reality of life is that you have to drop the world that you carry in your mind. Sometimes, people are so frustrated with the present situations of their life that they tend to create their dream life into their mind, and run away from the real event happening in their life. This keeps them from solving the real issues of life.

For example, there are many couples who lose their partners (spouse passing away) or they part ways! Especially women with children who part ways in marriage, when such people meet their ex partner on the way, they express disappointment, anger, frustration. They feel miserable, victimized, and burdened with all the financial responsibility on them and their children. They forget to move on. If you can create perfection out of what you already have in your life, you no longer have to live in your dreams, and you can have more pleasures out of, what you already have in your life.

Life is all about understanding. With life, your understanding towards it should grow simultaneously.

Stop putting your life on hold. If you keep looking at other's story, you can never move on. I raised my kid single handedly. I had nothing to fall back on. So I was willing to move on with a strong force towards creating a beautiful life on my own. That is the reason why I run a show that 'makes ordinary stories extraordinary'. People living an ordinary day to day life will definitely have a story within them that is extraordinary. My dear friend lost her husband few years ago, she has two kids. I met her sometime back. She had no financial support. She had to make it work on her own. And she did! Today, as I look at her, I feel empowered and powerful.

Let me now share the most powerful and intriguing fact.

My Mona-Vated MOMENT is

'Conception of my Book Mona-Vated'.

The very essence of Womanhood is my Mona-Vated Moment

& A MONA-VATED LIFE

This book is dedicated to all the empowered women and the powerful journeys that they undertook. May they all lead by example.

Chapter – 22
Letters to GOD

~ Unexpressed Emotions will never die. They are buried alive and will come forth later in uglier ways ~

SIGMUND FREUD

From very early on, I use to take out a special time to write a 'Letter to God' each day. I always felt that someone somewhere is listening to me! The Letters were big way to communicate with my subconscious mind. Yes, we all have tons and tons of beliefs stored in our subconscious mind. All of it is inaccessible and unknown to us. Psychologists have proven this for long years that those beliefs, memories always seek a way out to express themselves. Some of them are easily released in Dreams while for most of us it is released through more Dynamic Activity in our Life.

My purpose to share this Chapter particularly is –to encourage all of you to have an honest Self-Expression in life. Each one of us goes through a cauldron of difficult emotions in life. And a lot of times, we have trouble finding a voice for this pain.

Some of you will push this pain beneath the carpet simply because it is so traumatic that you don't want to face it. While others release this pain by resorting to activities such as Drinking, Smoking, rigorous physical work-out, extreme sports, drugs, etc. Let us assume that a child went through a traumatic experience of child molestation while he/she is just 5. Unaware of the emotion and inability to handle it will make the child aggressive, may be short tempered, extremely hyper or extreme recluse. The same child will grow and indulge in activity that involves aggression, life endangering situations or even as subtle as painting but he will paint only that which he experienced in childhood.

My Mind is a Subtle Body. It stores tons and tons of information. Events that cause us extreme pain are in fact pushed deep down in our subconscious mind. Here, Self-Expression becomes Necessary and Integral part of our Life. The moment you choose an act of Self-Expression and Self-Discovery, you will release the same traumatic or unpleasant emotion in a pleasant and healthy manner. This must be started very early in life. It is challenging to change our Emotional Set or Patterns as we grow older. So always choose activities and even encourage your children to find their way of expressing feelings. This will help them create a very suitable climate where their personalities can grow and flourish.

I am going to point out to a form of Expression that came to me in early childhood.

"WRITING"

Those were the days when we did not have any emails or texting. We all expressed our feelings through some pieces of writing. Sending Letters or telegrams were the only means of communication with others located at distant lands. I still have some letters that my friends sent to me. These letters always imbibe the energy of the person and the moment. Since it was all written with your own hand; it carried a special significance. Even when I read the letters now, I can associate with the hand-writing, the state of mind and complete expression of a being!

This was a time when I was left in India all by myself. My journey in Spirituality had begun in full swing. My daily meditations gave me profound insights about Life but one of the messages that was delivered very strongly was 'Start Writing'. I was asked to channelize my energy into 'Writing'. Since I had started visiting Botanical Garden, nature provided me the most perfect setting to write. I use to write all day long while sitting under the tree.

These were the days when I wrote Loads of Letters to GOD!

All that I needed was to express and put it down on paper. All my anger, fear, frustration, resentment were directly transferred on the piece of paper. Although many of us have doubt about our writing but the truth is – 'We are all Writers'.

I am not asking all of you to becomes 'Writers'; instead Write only to Express your point of View.

How do you feel at this point of time?

What makes you feel that way?

What can you do about the situation?

All these questions are simple ways to express your inner most conflict or even a desire. I choose to write all of it in form of 'Letters' where I expressed my feelings to the Universal Consciousness. I started my letters as 'Dear God, I am feeling XYZ…'

I was filled with emotions and frustrations as I started writing but eventually when I ended the chapter, I realized that all my burdens or heavy emotional states just vanished. It seemed as if I was releasing myself from the Past. I was setting myself Free in those precious moments of writing. That is when I realized the 'Power of Writing'.

The real transformation happened when I was able to see another perspective while being in the same situation. Till now, I was able to look at only one point of view. But as we write, we get a bird's eye view. We are able to understand from the frame of mind of others involved. Thus we always see a larger picture.

I was willing to Forget the Situation; Forgive Myself and Forgive Others!

I was Moving Ahead in Life

Writing played a Key Role in my Process of Transformation.

I was always inclined towards Solutions instead of emphasizing on Problems. I wanted to let go!

I might not share the same relationship with people who induced sadness in my life. But I always wanted to establish Peace in my Heart. We should always wish for a Peaceful Closure with

People especially those with whom we hold some kind of grudges. So that whenever we remember them, we connect to the goodness inside them!

Resentment is like Cancer. It grows slowly and silently. Before you know, it has already caused so much of harm and deterioration inside. Always work towards processes that will help you release the repressed emotions.

Letters to God is a Great Way to Release what is Not Required in your Life!

All my Letters revolved around my Ex-Husband, our circumstances, accepting what has happened and finally letting go of my Emotional Baggage.

~ Follow your Inner Moonlight; don't hide the Madness ~

Allen Ginsberg

The result was phenomenal. The more I wrote, the more I felt deep Love for people around. I had grown more compassionate. Solutions had started to appear as I wrote the problems on a piece of paper.

Today, as I conduct multiple programs on Law of Attraction, I ask people to write their goals and visions on a piece of paper. Studies and surveys have proved that the goals that we have written are more Attainable and Achievable. Every time you see that piece of paper, your goal gets deeply embedded in your Mind and Body. Make writing a part of your daily life. Even today, if I want to create something or express myself completely, I write a Letter to God.

One of the biggest Lessons that I imparted in my Son was writing down a letter each day where he expresses his Gratitude for everything around. When we are Grateful for our Surroundings, we automatically sow seeds for more beautiful things to come in our life.

~ If the only prayer you say in your life is 'Thank You,' that would suffice' ~

Meister Eckhart

Gratitude means thankfulness, counting your blessings, noticing simple pleasures and acknowledging everything that you receive. When you empower a young child with such a big tool, you instill a feeling of Positivity, Well-Being and Enthusiasm for the rest of his/her Life!

Gratitude is the only tool that will shift your focus from what your life lacks to the abundance that is already present.

Make a daily list of things for which you are Grateful. Follow it like a ritual for Life. Eventually you will realize that you are making greater progress towards achieving your personal goals. You will constantly look for good even in unpleasant situations.

Write

Release

And Create More....

Chapter 23
Powerful Tool to Achieve your Goals

This is a chapter that emphasizes on the most powerful instrument available to a man, that will help him reach his Goals Instantly.

If you are committed to winning at work and succeeding in life, then I highly suggest that you use this to empower yourself!

Stop putting the Rest of your Life on Hold.

Stop waiting for People who will come and help you fulfill your Dream.

It is Time you take the full responsibility of your Life.

Let us begin with some facts –

25% of people abandon their Goals after one week.

60% of people abandon them within six months.

Only 5% of those who stick by their long term goals succeed.

Another 10% of people will constantly work towards their Goals after they go through a setback in life.

A Researcher named Dr. Gail Matthews, psychology professor at Dominican University at California, did a study on Goal-Setting with 267 participants. She found that 42% are more likely to achieve their goals by just writing them down.

I have found this to be true in my own experience. As mentioned in previous chapter, writing not only helped me release my repressed emotions and also facilitated in finding solutions.

My purpose of sharing these facts was to help you understand that Life is very dynamic. Every day we have ample tasks that cloud our mind. Amidst all the confusion and stress which has unconsciously become a part of our daily life, we tend to lose focus.

When you write your Goals down every day, you program your subconscious mind correctly. Every research has proven that programming the subconscious mind is essential to achieving the success you want in life. The day your subconscious mind is highly programmed, you are able to move faster, longer, with more efficiency and dedication than ever before.

Your Mind will make YOU Virtually Unstoppable!

You will do all the tasks with the highest level of Integrity, Commitment and Power!

The Most Efficient way to Program the Mind in this manner is 'Writing your Goals/Visions'

Let me share some more insights on how does this process work-

First thing in the morning, write down the 10 most important goals.

Step 1: It will clear the confusion or doubt and will program the mind correctly.

Step 2: When done on a consistent and regular basis, you will be able to move towards these goals extremely easily. This is because they will be at the forefront of your mind.

Step 3: Your Mind will always keep reminding you that these are important tasks. You will place more emphasis on it. Your mind will make you feel a sense of urgency and propel you towards these goals.

Step 4: Your Mind will always push aside that which is not facilitating these Goals. So you are continuously moving towards the targeted goals without getting wavered by external influences.

> *Do this Goal-Setting Exercise for 2-3 weeks minimum in order to see substantial results in life.*

Even a small amount of attention each day is enough to turn any goal into reality!

I have seen it time and again in my own life. In fact I am more and more convinced that to live and be successful and have a fulfilled life, we must WRITE our goals. That includes daily, weekly, monthly, yearly, short-term, long term goals and even life goals.

If you want to move up from mediocre to excellence in your living, then you need to develop the DISCIPLINE of writing out your goals daily.

Don't just speak out your Goals.

Don't just Visualize them.

Instead take a pen and paper and take the TIME to write them.

Here are some simple examples of how you could write your Goals---

- I am happy because I exercised 20 minutes today and ate organic meals at the proper time. I feel Healthy and full of Vitality.
- I am happy because I spent 10 minutes in Silence, calming my Mind and channelizing my Energies in right direction.
- I am happy because I have surrounded myself with 10 key people who support me in my endeavors, are honest and disciplined.

- I am happy because I have made an additional allowance of Rs. 50,000 in past 2 months. I am on the path of making much more in next two months.

A Day with a Goal is a Day that is whole!

Chapter 24
Choose Happiness

We are stepping into a time where more and more people are moving towards Conscious Living. We are diverting our attention from the regular hustle-bustle to various therapies that gives us peace of Mind. Many of us feel inclined towards learning these Alternative Therapies and Processes. Any of the complimentary or alternative therapies are an excellent tool to provide Balance in Life.

Individuals resorting to Healthy Lifestyle, Yoga, Meditation, Reiki and other Healing Modalities have experienced physical, mental and spiritual gains. These alternative therapies also change the outlook towards life. We are able to overcome our fears, emotional trauma, stress, depression and even chronic illness. I have personally learnt Reiki, Theta Healing and some of other Healing Therapies. They all have added some or the other value in my life. But one thing which remained unchanged throughout my Life was – 'Focusing on Joy and Happiness in Life'

This chapter is focused on 'understanding' the importance of 'Happiness'

As humans, our only pursuit is to move towards Happiness in life. Whatever we may be doing or being or seeing, we only strive towards Happiness within and then around us.

~ Aristotle pondered the causes and impact of happiness as long ago as 322 BC. He suggested that pursuit of Happiness was an essential part of being human, and a goal in itself ~

All our logics and reasons tell us that Happiness is within our reach, that we will not be satisfied unless we attain the state of everlasting happiness. Even our Intuition tells us the same. Happiness is self-evident and needs no outside confirmation. We see it in children; we experience it in momentary glimpses. It is this search for happiness that takes a person to a temple, or church or mosque, a priest, a guru, to the stock market, the casino, the battlefield or a lonely place on the mountain top. Even when we are going and attending life growth programs, we are basically making efforts to bring more happiness in our life.

Finally, we all know, Nothing is More Precious than Happiness!

All your efforts for Self-Transformation and reading Self-Help Books will allow you to blossom immediately. You will be freed from all the subtle influences of the past and from all the anxieties of the future. But as I mentioned before, 'Life is Dynamic'. It will always give you reasons to be pulled back into worries, apprehensions and negativity.

Living in the here and now is the permanent address for Happiness.

I have come to this conclusion from my own life experiences. No matter how many therapies I learn or endless workshops that I conduct, I still have my weak moments in Life. I still feel sadness and recluse many a times. But I always push buttons of Happiness even in the most deteriorating situation. It might take time to gather your Energy but once you make it a part of your being, you will always operate from the Zone of Happiness and Joy.

You can feel free to use any alternative therapy, healing modality, or any re-creational activity that induces a state of Happiness and Well-Being.

San Francisco State University, 2009 conducted a study demonstrating that experiential purchases, such as a meal out or theatre tickets, result in greater well-being than material possessions. These experiences tend to satisfy higher order needs, specifically the need for social connectedness and vitality- a feeling of being alive.

Conclusion drawn: Buying Experiences, not Possessions, Leads to Greater Happiness!

Yet another study performed at the Institute of HeartMath, researchers discovered that positive feelings and emotions will have a profound impact on physiology. Feelings of Love, Happiness and Appreciation had a measurable and significant impact on the beating patterns of the heart, making the heart beats more coherent and regular.

Let me share with you another study that was conducted on 1200 Males by The John Hopkins School Of Medicine. They found that those who experienced depression were twice as likely to develop coronary heart disease or have a heart attack 15 years later.

The consistent theme of modern research is that happiness, contentment, joy, love, appreciation and positive moods have a positive effect on our mental and physical health. On the contrary, negative moods, depression, anxiety and stress consistently have a detrimental effect on our health.

The link between Happiness and Health has been signed, sealed and delivered.

Some simple tips that one must follow for the everyday doze of happiness:

- Eat Healthy, all day, every day!

- Use a positive Exercise Regime to keep you feeling good.

- Keep your Mind mentally Active at all the time.

- Always talk Highly of others and Mindful of your thoughts.

- Be Goal Oriented – By Simply Writing your Goals each day.

- Have a Positive System of Feelings in your Body.

- Only Associate yourself with Positive Images and Thoughts which will help you be in Balanced State.

Today, there are countless studies that have demonstrated that Happiness is the Real Medicine. And this Happiness will be found everywhere if we look around.

~ If you want happiness for an hour – take a nap. If you want happiness for a day – go fishing. If you want happiness for a month – get married. If you want happiness for a year – inherit a fortune. If you want happiness for a lifetime – help others ~

Chinese proverb

Life gives us endless opportunities to experience happiness. Even if these opportunities bring temporary discomfort, it is fine. Think about a time in life when you went through a tough but rewarding experience. Every experience that you remember of will be the same. There was great anxiety, feeling of failure but you end up achieving something even in the most serious life situations. Either you open yourself to new opportunities, become a little wiser or gain a greater sense of self-confidence after emerging from turmoil.

It just shows that the state of happiness is constant. It is just our way of looking at it. I see Beauty and Happiness in the most imperfect beings as well. One should embrace and accept all aspects of life – sadness, frustration, pain, failure and happiness. These entire elements combine together to give us a Balanced, Fulfilling and truly Happy Experience.

The secret is to step from the State of Happiness to the State of Wholeness. When you step into the State of Wholeness, you grow stronger, wiser and more whole as an individual. Rather than trying to hide from adversities, we embrace them because deep inside we know that the same situations will make us passionate, motivated, versatile, confident and capable –

Adding more meaning and deeper fulfillment to our lives.

Laugh at your own mistakes and learn from them.

Joke about your troubles and gather strength from them.

Have fun with the challenges you face and then conquer them!
Anything that you do in life will ask you to step out of your comfort zone. You may indulge in unusual things, or usual things, something big or small. But in order to make a real change in life, you need to expand your comfort zone. Change your perspective for yourself. Instead of sticking to old and comfortable ways of living, try to mix up things. The moment you break free from inner resistance and fear that holds you back; you move towards Happiness and Wholeness.

Add spark to your life each day. When you do things differently, you discover tons of new and exciting things. This automatically re-fuels your consciousness. People who do this successfully are able to make a tremendously positive impact and even find more opportunities – both at work and outside work.

As Sri Aurobindo puts it "It is a mistake to think that by fearing or being unhappy you can progress. Fear is always a feeling to be rejected, because what you fear is just the thing that is likely to come to you. Fear attracts the object of fear. Unhappiness weakens strength and lays one more open to the causes of unhappiness."

Make Happiness an expression of Gratitude. Be thankful that Life is allowing you to feel it. Share that Happiness with someone that you love. Be generous with your Success and help someone else out who is struggling with their own tragedy.

Chapter 25
Get Money Flowing to you
~ Real Riches are the Riches Possessed Inside. ~
B.C. FORBES

Money, it is such a heavy topic for many and it was for me too at one point.

In this chapter, allow me to talk about our Relationship with Money.

Relationship??

You might be thinking what I mean by Relationship!

We all have heard about relationship with others or self.

Do you know we also share a relationship with money?

We might think of money as evil, good, bad, it may be in abundance or there might be a lack of it... And we experience many emotions around it.

Try and finish these sentences for me please…

Money doesn't grow on …. ??

We got to work hard to get …. ??

Greedy people are …. ??

Money is the root to all …. ??

Did you hear yourself say….

Money doesn't grow on trees

We got to work hard to get ahead

Greedy people are dishonest

Money is the root to all evil

And of course there are many other sentences that might cross your mind.

I am not saying it is true for you or everyone but many people carry such beliefs. What we hear in our early age is what we start to believe! For instance I remember my mother repeating 'we cannot afford it' again and again. Now I am not saying it is right or wrong to say that. In her situation, she knew that was the best thing to do.

I still remember an incident. I was 8 year old when we had my dad's sister visit us from another town with her daughter who was just a year older than me. In our family we had a tradition, which is still practiced in Indian Families. When we have guests visiting us, we never let them leave empty handed. So we all went out to buy gifts for my relatives. My mom selected a pretty frock – dress for my cousin. I sat there watching her, while she looks into the fitting of new dress. I felt a deep desire to have a new dress too so I insisted that my mom should get me one too. My mom kept denying while my aunt offered to buy me one. Since my mother had deep embedded beliefs about integrity and guest hosting, she didn't allow my aunt to pay. Finally she bought the dress for me herself.

I was super excited to have a brand new dress. Since I was the youngest in the family, I always wore dresses that were worn by my elder sisters and passed on to me as they grew older. For me this was an exciting moment.

Perfect white dress!

I was told to wait for few days before I wear it. So I waited patiently, looking forward to that day. Dreaming, thinking and imagining myself in my white dress.

A couple of days later, my mom went to return the dress. I was completely shocked. Later I was told that 'the dress was bought so that your aunt doesn't pay for it. But now we must return it because it is expensive and we can't afford it'.

My heart was shattered into pieces!

I was not allowed to say anything. The decision was forced on me but of course an 8 year old made up her own story around it and that was –

We can't afford things and

Many other beliefs around my Worthiness and Money Emerged.

That pattern drove my life for many years. When I came to Canada, I got a good paying job within 20 days as shared with you before but I never learnt 'how to spend money'. I became a great saver. I gave away all the monitory control to my father. I worked hard to make money but never really tried managing it as my belief around worthiness stopped me.

Even when I could afford good decently price clothes, I always found myself in thrift stores, and would end up buying used clothes. This was not by chance. It was a pattern and a habit that was embedded within me since early childhood.

There is nothing right or wrong about buying used clothes. In fact it is a matter of personal choice. But I am here trying to emphasis on the mindset of spending and thinking that – You don't deserve NEW!

Same pattern repeated in my married life for long years.

My Mona-Vated Moment came when I went to work and needed some professional pictures clicked. For which I needed a new business suit. Guess where I found myself again – THRIFT STORE.

As I was trying outfit in a fitting room something came over and I asked myself.. WHAT AM I DOING?

FOR HOW LONG WILL I COMPROMISE ON MY SELF WORTH?

What kind of clients do I want?

I had all those questions running through my mind.

I wasn't questioning the energy that used clothes would have but personally I was tired of wearing OLD. I just rushed out of that store and without giving it a second thought I straight went to the stores Downtown. I entered the most expensive store and bought myself an 800 dollars business suit. When I came back home I kept questioning myself on what I had done. That is literally the one month rent for many people around. I had recurrent thoughts of returning the suit. But one thing was clear it is NOW or NEVER.

I am not suggesting that you go out and buy the most expensive clothes. Even as a Mother I never bought everything my son had asked for but I became very conscious of my own beliefs. I made sure that when I engage into a dialogue with my son, I should only impart him positive and empowering beliefs around money. **Every word that I used was coming from a place of Abundance instead of feeling of Lacking.**

Just check your own thoughts and feelings when it comes to Money. You might find this chapter longer than other chapters. In my tours, coaching, workshops, seminars and speaking engagements, the biggest questions always revolves around MONEY and how to ATTRACT MORE.

Often, I take my clients deeper and allow them to see their RELATIONSHIP with money. Then it becomes very clear to them. Money is always knocking at our door; it is our own thoughts and feelings that stop us from welcoming it in our life.

Just imagine that these money blocks have growing roots and they penetrate deeper and deeper into our life as the years pass by.

Most of it is unconscious beliefs taken from the conditioning of your parents, friends, teachers and society.

If you introspect about it, you might feel bad because these are the things you haven't been given a chance to logically process or form a belief yourself. For example, given a choice today, I would never choose to believe that 'I am not worthy of money or abundance in life'.

Unfortunately, these non-required beliefs attach themselves to your subconscious and drastically impact your reality. Just as mentioned earlier in this chapter. Now, whatever these blocks are and under what ever circumstances they entered your body. You don't have to dig into your memory and wonder HOW or WHY?

You must only be ready to begin creating a world filled with Abundance, Riches, Wealth, Money, Prosperity and Joy.

It might sound like too much of 'hard work' right now. But it is not!

There is a secret to getting everything you ever wanted in life. And this secret is really simple. May be you have heard about it or understand it already but are unable to use it in practical life. I will not share the principle secret with you as it can only be imparted in an experiential manner during my training programs. But I will surely give you a glimpse of how beautiful this journey is once you know the secret.

Everything that comes into physical reality is first 'formless' – it is actually floating all around us. You can tap into this formless substance through your mind. It is as simple as passing by a café. You instantly stop as you see a freshly baked muffin displayed on the shelf. You enter the café and immediately place an order. You simply placed an order for what you want. We do that every day. Isn't it?

This is exactly how you place an order from Universe. You just ask for what you want.

What happens next?

Now, by simply holding an idea in your mind; circumstances will cause it to appear in your physical world. Just as the fresh muffin comes to you physically and you savior the taste and aroma of it in your mouth. Too often, you are thinking of what you don't want – which causes the thing you don't want to actually happen and then you wonder WHY things don't change year after year. Change your thoughts and you change your world!

So always look deeper to understand – where exactly is your MINDSET?

Do you have a PROSPERITY CONSCIOUSNESS?

Or

POVERTY CONSCIOUSNESS?

You can continue to re-create the same life over and over again or you can truly commit yourself to having a Powerful Financial Future in your hands. You can DESIGN it the way you want it to. Once you release your money sabotage and tap into the infinite power, there will be nothing that can Stop or Block your Path.

Let me share a very short story here to make it little clearer.

There was this king who had a big giant mansion and all the money in the world that he could imagine. He married a very simple, mediocre lady. She was someone who was stuck questioning her worthiness of living a royal life. As she was overlooking the mansion from her bedroom door, the king approached and asked the reason for her sadness. She replied, I don't belong here, it is awkward for me and I would like to give away all this.

King smiled and agreed. He replied, 'if that is what you desire I will give away all of it. But even if I do this, it will all come back to me!

BECAUSE

It is not what I have but what I KNOW…

The moment you start working on your relationship with money, life will start showing you results. Everything will start falling into the place on its own.

You probably might have heard the stories of people who inherit a big amount of money or win lottery and go back to same status quo in few months. They lose all that they gain and come to streets. Simultaneously, there are also stories of people who went bankrupt and still rise from their ashes. They made it big again. Donald Trump is one big example here.

Why do you think is the reason?

IT IS NOT WHAT WE HAVE BUT WHAT WE KNOW!

It is hard to build wealth when deep down, we view money as an obstacle. Growing up, we hear many views around money. Most of them acclaim that 'money isn't something to be embraced'. All my childhood, I heard only one sentence. 'We cannot afford it'. So I rarely saw money as a positive thing. I always saw money as being needed or we wanted it but it never wanted us.

Now, there is a big difference in these two statements. We know that we want money to fulfill our basic needs. This statement was clearly stated. But since we also had this secret unwanted evil belief around money deeply hidden in some corner; we had a serious conflict/dilemma whether money receiving is finally good or bad?

Not knowing what to do and how to resolve the internal conflict, we become more and more desperate to go after money. We continuously keep thinking about making money and chasing it. Finally it becomes a never ending chase in fact a **TIRING CHASE.**

I feel blessed that I gave myself permission to understand this SECRET. Opportunities always knocked at my door and Money never crossed my mind because everything came to me very easily and effortlessly. Yes I lost it all when I went through my struggles with my Divorce as mentioned before. But I had worked on myself and my relationship with money. So I attracted a comfortable life all over again with ease and grace. I was easily able to afford holiday vacations for me and my son. I bought my dream car. I am living a very comfortable life now.

It is not about living the life of millionaire or billionaire. It is actually a 'Contented Life' which brings the feeling of Abundance. There is nothing wrong in wishing for more money or making tons of money. I think that is an excellent idea. We can surely have a goal of earning a better lifestyle than what we are living and more opportunities for us and our loved ones. To have because the more we can earn for ourselves, we can open more opportunities for others. Maybe jobs, contracts, being able to give back to community and helping with a meaningful cause.

Sometimes it is also about what we are doing to make the money? If your source of income is coming from something that you are not enjoying doing then of course it will feel like a drag but if you are absolutely doing what you love and what you offer is from the place of love.. MONEY will just simply follow you everywhere you go because it is not from the place of I HAVE TO but rather from the place of I WANT TO …

Be of service to others whether you are in Job or in business for yourself always ask yourself How is what I am offering going to change the other person's life, be it a product or service. When we put other people's needs first even the UNIVERSE comes forward 1000 steps to align us with our purpose and what we have to offer.

This is very important to note for all those who are self employed -- always pay yourself FIRST. Most of us end up paying the bills, paying salaries to hired employees, pooling money for business expenses and take the left over home if any is left. Learn to pay yourself first even its small percentage but that is the first step to SELF WORTHINESS AND DESERVING OF.

As much as I have come long ways when it comes to money and my relationship with money but I still have issues with money that show up at times in my thought process and how I see money. I get mad at it and blame it at times when something does not go right. That is when I remind myself money is just money, my day to day life and what I vision for myself and my goals are more important to me. I am not saying it is not important to get you what you want but money is just a tool at its core.

In the end best way I can sum up by these beautiful amazing words by **_Author Nina Wise-_** *"Our longing for freedom cannot be satisfied by cars, houses , diamonds, private jets or offshore bank accounts or caviar; by miniature computers or mighty weapons. Our longing for freedom can only be satisfied by recognizing that we are each sufficient as we are and that what feeds us has nothing do with what we buy and everything to do with an inherent vitality of the soul"*

Chapter 26
LAW OF ATTRACTION
--- a blessing in disguise

All along the misery, sorrow, agony or hurt, the only thing that remained synchronous were my **Vibrations!**

They were perfectly aligned with the Universe. More so after I started Meditating.

What We Think; What We Feel; What We Do…. Everything is aligned with Universe and attracts likewise. This is an undisturbed law. It does not run as per the whims and fancies of our mind. It is just there irrespective of whether I accept this statement or not!

Let me give you a small example. I am planting a seed of watermelon and I suddenly get surprised when I see oranges growing out of it. Than the first statement will be—

OMG! I never asked for this ~~

I always wanted Watermelon. Why did I not get what I wanted?

Now think, how did this happen?

The plant will give us oranges because we sowed the seed for oranges and not watermelon. We don't realize that the thoughts we are carrying are the same seeds that we are planting in Universe. So remember, when I spoke about my low self-esteem and being called 'Kali' over many years. But one day, as I learnt about the tanning salon, I experienced a complete transformation inside. I instantly gave a message to Universe that I am worth of every appreciation and compliments. Just because I planted the seed of 'Self-Worth' and 'Being Beautiful', everything started to change!

The more I said to myself that I am beautiful, the more appreciation I received from people around. So that's when I started to do my own little study around law of Attraction.

How does it work?

What does it do?

5% of population makes most of the money and they are happy while 95% of population is not!

What makes these 5% more receiving? What is that extra bit that they are doing or thinking?

Suddenly, I realized that our thoughts play a big role in the universe and there is a big process of creation. I started to travel and meet people who have genuinely worked in this field. They are the Masters such as Bob Proctor, Michael Beckwith, John Assaraf, Michael Gerber, David Riklan, Bernard Bouchard, Mark Victor Hansen, Brian Tracy, Tony Robbins and T Harvker. At that time, I was making really good money with my Real Estate Business. So I was able to talk to these Masters, spend time with them and learn the dynamics of it. Everything was reaching me very beautifully. I had a thought and it would come into reality.

Let me share another example from my Life. I wanted a BMW convertible. I did not know the real working of Law of Attraction but the only thing I did was –

I started pretending that my present car was my new BMW!

In fact I would go to the gas station and ask the guy to fill gas into my BMW. He would look puzzled because technically I was driving a Honda car. However, I did not let my thoughts waver. They were perfectly aligned with my desire to own a new BMW Convertible.

You create your thoughts &

You create your reality.

The most important is to set yourself free from other's thoughts as they continuously interfere with your process of Law of Attraction!

If I would have been bothered by what people are thinking when I pretended to be sitting in my BMW; I would have never seen my dream as a reality. But the real challenge is to set yourself free from surrounding and submerge in your dream!

Within a month, I was able to generate enough funds from just one deal and I finally got the BMW for myself.

My Mona-Vated Moment.

**I realized that the Universe does not understand the difference between mental and physical images. If we have installed a mental image, The Universe has to fill in the gap.
So whatever i thought, the Universe would respond.**

Let me remind you here, a lot of people say we asked for things but it did not come true. That is because their thoughts are scattered. Whereas I focused my thoughts in only one positive frame.

Where the focus goes, it grows!

Even my son created a project called 'To Think is to Create'. I was even teaching him how our thoughts create reality!

Now that I was working with Law of Attraction principles so closely; everything that I ever wanted was flooding in! This was before I moved back to India. The process was gradually growing on me and I felt a deep desire to Master It.

When I came to India, I realized that Universe was preparing me for something bigger. That is why I was meeting all these people. Everything was gone from my life. I had nothing to fall back on, except law of Attraction.

While meditating in my home in Delhi, my mother conveyed many messages. It seemed as if Universe was helping me understand the deeper realities of Life. But the most powerful message was –

'Work on Law of Attraction'

There are many Laws of Universe. But my journey is to only work on the eternal 'Law of Attraction'. Master it and Teach Others. That's when I started doing my workshops in Delhi. When people came to my class, they realized that Law of Attraction happens much faster when we align ourselves with other law of Universe such as –

The Law of Thinking

The Law of Supply

The Law of Attraction

The Law of Receiving

The Law of Increase

The Law of Compensation

The Law of Non-Resistance

The Law of Forgiveness

The Law of Sacrifice

The Law of Obedience

And finally....

The Law of Success

Even though I knew about all *these* principles much before. But it was majorly my own life experiences that taught me the practicality of it.

The more I learned about my own thoughts, the more faster things started to happen in my life. I needed people to understand this. Most of the people feel frustrated as they keep intent, follow some principles but when nothing happens, they give up!

That's where I wanted to intervene and tell them that unless they align themselves with the other 11 Laws mentioned above, the process of Law of Attraction will not work!

Yes, it is very important to know them.

The 3 day workshop has been devised in a way that the first two days are only dedicated to understand and imbibe the other principles of Life.

In these 3 days, I am just showing them the mirror. I don't intend to teach or preach or lecture people. I just draw the energy out of them. It is not a student- teacher relationship. Instead I want people to tap into their own experiences.

Allow them to see their life closely and experience their AHA moments or Mona-Vated Moments in full bloom.

This is the Art of Motivating Self!

Yet another dimension that is given much needed attention is – Working on The Inner Child!

How many of us believe that the perceptions or beliefs made during childhood leave a great impact on life as we grow old?

Certain pleasant or unpleasant experiences leave a profound mark on our Mind-Body. These beliefs could be around Money, Relationship, Health, Wealth or Self. So we look into these beliefs deeply on the second day of workshop.

Do not question – How will Law of Attraction Work?

Instead ask – Why do I want this?

Questioning the WHY is the first step and most important!

We were born with everything. A child has all the ability to manifest in his innocence. Sadly, as we grow, we condition our mind with disbeliefs and apprehensions. So I want them to remove their doubts and beliefs in these 3 days.

I am willing to help my participants in every way in order to give them their wings!

They fly high and experience the life in full spring!

Chapter 27
The Power of Your Thoughts

There's a Child in All of Us! No matter what age we may say we are or how old someone looks they started out as a child…

That Child Lives Inside!

~*LOVE YOUR INNER CHILD~*

As you connect to the beautiful inner child, miracles happen. Life may have hit you with the saddest or the most disastrous moments. And it may continue doing this. But never give up on being happy. Never ignore the Child inside you!

I was going through a lot of pain but I laughed, I always had my inner child shining…. Not Childish but Childlike …

In all the chapters that you read so far, you must have realized that there was one such moment where I let my guards down to find that small but substantial moment of happiness or positivity! That is why I called these as 'Mona-Vated Moments'. Here I allowed my Inner Child to speak again. I gave her a box of crayons and asked her to paint again.

When you are traveling on your life course, trying to overcome all the odds, working on the impossible; it is best to have Fun, Laugh and Smile on the journey. This will make your Journey a lot easier and faster.

My 3 Day Workshop Specifically emphasizes on 'Awakening the Inner Child'. Everything is Possible if you Look through the

Eyes of a Child. And that is what I will ask you to do in these 3 days.

My exercises will bring back the Inner Child from your kindergarten days. He is the one who knew ---**'Everything is Attainable!'**

Life is like a Lego. Pick up the pieces and start building. If it doesn't feel right, knock it down and re build - SIMPLE.

But Yes, add FUN & EXCITEMENT To Your GAME... Be CHILDLIKE...

You are RESPONSIBLE for your LIFE. You designed your own rules in the game. And then, it becomes your responsibility to follow your own structures. If you win, you take the credit. But if you loose, you easily Blame somebody else for your Dysfunction!

That is Wrong.

Your Life is the Result of YOUR Decisions and Choices.

The objective is to neither Blame nor be a Victim to the situation. Rather feel the Responsibility.

For humans, it's easy to blame than looking inwards and ask yourself 'What do I need to Change within Me; in order to Change the Situation.'

Let me Narrate a Story to you ---

There was a Girl named Penny. She had a lot of sweets all of which she treasured. Penny made a new friend called Nickel. He was a sweet lover. He also had something that he always treasured. He owned loads and loads of marbles. One day Nickel realized that he couldn't hold his temptation any longer and asked Penny if she would trade ALL of her sweets for the ALL the marbles that he had. She agreed to it. The deal was sealed. That night Penny slept very peacefully and calmly just like any other night. However, Nickel spent the whole night being restless and couldn't sleep at all thinking- what if Penny did not give ALL OF HER SWEETS TO ME .... !!!

Do you know Why??? Why did he question that all night to himself?

It is because he kept a few of his favorite marbles aside even though the deal was to trade ALL FOR ALL ....

You see, when we question or doubt the integrity of the other; we are actually doubting our own Integrity and Authenticity.

It is not about other person at all!

It is always about ourselves.

Whether we can trust OURSELVES or not!

If we are hiding something we think whole world is hiding something. When we are not honest; we think that the other is always dishonest. When we don't give our 100%; we think others are not giving their 100%.

Life is like a RECIPE ~~

If you put salt; you can't expect pepper!

Sugar will lead to a sweet dish; lemon will lead to a savory dish.

Nothing more.. Nothing less ...

What you put in your own recipe called LIFE will be reflected back!

The interesting part is --

Recipes can be altered, changed or even modified at any time!

Just ask yourself --

How is your Recipe going to be different from others ????

Our choices create our life. If we do not like something; JUST MAKE A DIFFERENT CHOICE!

I did make some not so great relationship decisions when I was younger but my Learnings have been far greater only because of these decisions.

Incredible things happen when you decide to take control instead of wondering -

'What the hell happened to me?'

Finally, we are all connected. There is no separation at soul level. So even when you don't feel connected to someone, let go of the person or situation. And feel the acceptance that Everyone is doing things to best of their ability!

My son taught me the best lesson of how he tried to do the BEST in one SITUATION.

Listen to yet another story--

One of the days at school, Paras saw few kids chatting in a group and they started throwing their change money away. They all had some extra pennies kept in their pockets. Since it was just extra change, they didn't feel it was worth keeping. So they literally started throwing the money. Paras, on the other hand understood the power of money and had enormous respect for it. He didn't let his OWN JUDGEMENTS or Judgements of OTHERS stop him. He went and picked up all the change, Blessed it, put it in his pocket and came home. We had a special place at home where Paras and me collect found money.

We thought that this is indeed a trigger for us that ABUNDANCE is all around! We just need to focus on it.

Later, he shared the incident with me and said, 'Every Penny counts. If we can respect and have a gratitude for every penny, nickels and dime, god will shower more'.

My son had revealed the biggest secret of 'Law of Attraction' --

Whatever we value in our life, it shows up more profoundly - Be it a Relationship, Money, Perfect Health!

This incident reminded me of all the inventories of Life --Relationships, Money, Self, Others, Health, Peace.

You can Desire anything in Life. Just ask yourself --How Much Did I Value It?

If you valued it intensely, if you are Grateful for what you have; you can live the most Fulfilling and Flourishing life ever! You are privileged and are doing a lot better than most of the world. There are those who have nothing at all.

Know that Abundance is all around you. We just have to capture it at each Moment!

A philosopher once quoted--

From Abundance, take Abundance and Abundance Still Remains!

So Let this be your Mantra from Now On -

'Where ever I turn; I am always surrounded by Abundance. All my Wishes and Needs are well taken care of'.

My journey with my Son has been so phenomenal that being a single mother was a boon to me! There was some level of apprehension whether or not I will be able to take care of my child. But his silence said it all.

He understood in ways that I would never expect a 9 years old or 12 year old to understand. Just when work and life were in great transition, we had to spend the entire month eating 1$ noodles each day for 30 days. Financial crisis and drastic changes in Life had not left any other option for us!

But together we could outgrow all these hassles of Life. Motherhood is a Spiritual Exploration unto itself.

Regardless of what I teach or how much I have worked on myself. I know that I'm still not perfect. Neither do I intend to be perfect!

We simply are living and experiencing this life in our own unique ways. My Situations in Life only made me stronger but not perfect.

I still go through my moments. I get hurt like everyone else, I have all kind of Emotional Moments to deal with like everyone else. I too get my mood swings just like everyone else. I cry to discharge my emotions.

The only difference between me and any other light worker is 'I choose to play the game of Life with a HAPPY FACE, LOVE, JOY, FORGIVENESS and PEACE!

I like to smile and laugh in spite of any pain and this is not because I like to hide my pain behind my smiles but I consciously choose not to worry about my pain and rather live each moment with glory.

When I take my last breath I want to make sure I had smile on my face and was making someone else smile. I want my son to remember me as HAPPY MOTHER ! !

Life is a constant and continuous journey.

With every incident, the mind is ignited and new learning's are served to us on a hot plate! These learning will always exist. So ending this book or chapter with perfect ending is just not possible.

I may be one of the rare Authors who will not give any Closure to this book as I am still on my journey and will continue to be on one as long as I live!

The only message that I derived out of my journey is --

~~ *Live with a purpose*

~~ *Leave behind the legacy*

~~ *Don't wait till everything is perfect. Just take steps towards your Vision, Purpose, Goals or Dream (even if it is risky steps)*

I always liked the Nike tag line 'JUST DO IT'

Always keep smiling and keep shining...

Whatever you say, Universe/God says YES to it.

We are all governed by FREE WILL.

So what we choose to BELIEVE actually becomes our TRUTH. And the mind goes to make that REALITY!

For instance, if I have a belief saying that I can't trust people. The Universe says "YES you are right. Now let me go and find those circumstances and situations where people are dishonest to you."

VERSUS

IF you say that I trust people and opportunities. God/Universe turns the table and sends you the Love and Support you need on your Journey.

This time again, Universe wants to emphasize that -- YES YOU ARE RIGHT!

Just remember that since Universe is saying YES TO EVERYTHING. And it is that SIMPLE!

You need to be careful about one thing

~~ Choose your Thoughts and Words Wisely for they are the Energy that Creates your Life ~~

Remember that there is no greater purpose than living each Moment to our Best! I see and hear so many stories where people feel lost because they never found their purpose of life.

The Only Purpose is to 'BE THE STAR IN OUR OWN LIFE STORY where we win a 'GRAMMY AWARD' every day, and we are honored with a NOBLE PRICE every moment'!

I'm not a writer and for the longest time I struggled with it. I thought to myself that either I have to be an amazing writer or someone has to write on my behalf in order to spread my message.

But my meditations and my mom's guidance told me that I don't need to be a good writer, or have perfect grammar. I just need to be ME and let the message of Love, Peace and Forgiveness spread through me.

No matter where you are or what circumstances hit you, please allow the Universe to work through you. Soon you would know the Purpose of why it happens in your Journey.

Life is truly a Blessing if we chose to believe that - ***then Life becomes a MIRACLE and has only Magical Moments in store for us ~!!~***

This wonderful Journey continues for me and all of you my lovely readers. Till the next time, keep Smiling and Keep Shinning.

Love
Mona Arora

Front cover photography :

        Sukh Janda jandaphotography.ca

Makeup and Hair Artist:

        Mindy Bansal & Ina Mander girlfriendzstudio7.com